THE PORTABLE BUSINESS WRITER

William Murdick

California University of Pennsylvania

Houghton Mifflin Company *Boston New York*

Senior Sponsoring Editor Suzanne Phelps Weir
Senior Associate Editor Janet Edmonds
Senior Project Editor Helen Bronk
Senior Production/Design Coordinator Jennifer Waddell
Senior Manufacturing Coordinator Sally Culler
Senior Marketing Manager Nancy Lyman

Cover design by Linda Manly Wade

Grateful acknowledgment is made to Edward Norwood and Rev. James B. Bailey for permission to quote their work and to the Modern Language Association of America for permission to reprint, in Chapter 16, the MLA Guidelines on Citing Sources from the World Wide Web.

Printed in the U.S.A.

Library of Congress Catalog Card Number: 98-72065

ISBN: 0-395-90921-X

123456789-FFG-02 01 00 99 98

CONTENTS

PREFACE

Overview

The Portable Business Writer is a comprehensive textbook for a first college course in business writing. Like the other books in Houghton Mifflin's *English Essentials* series, *The Portable Business Writer* is a lean, inexpensive volume that counters the rising cost of textbooks without sacrificing key coverage or quality. Although it is stripped of nonessential content, this book nevertheless offers twenty-six chapters covering traditional and new topics for today's courses in business writing.

Important and familiar topics covered in this book include the following:

formatting business documents
developing an effective style and tone
handling good news, bad news, and delicate messages
making personal requests
writing internal and external proposals
conducting and presenting survey research and library research
writing routine and long reports
creating effective sales letters
planning and delivering oral presentations
putting together an impressive resume and cover letter

As an up-to-date text, *The Portable Business Writer* also takes into account the dramatic changes that have occurred in the professional workplace during the past decade. Major developments include the computerization of modern offices, increasing numbers of women and minorities serving in managerial positions or as successful independent entrepreneurs, and the rise of the global economy. Zooming in on these developments, this book includes chapters on the following topics:

using e-mail
conducting electronic job searches
avoiding biased policy and languages
communicating across cultures

To broaden its coverage further, *The Portable Business Writer* looks at writing problems that arise in the corporate community, in the small business environment, and in the private life of a college student.

A Business Philosophy and a Writing Philosophy

The Portable Business Writer has a business philosophy and a writing philosophy. The foundation of the business philosophy is the idea that people engaged in business communications are rarely enemies. The purpose of most business writing, then, is not to challenge a foe, but to meld purpose and action among colleagues, or to obtain cooperation from someone outside the organization. This idea affects not only the tone of effective business communications, but also the strategy. *The Portable Business Writer* teaches methods for achieving one's writing purpose while satisfying the needs of the audience. At the same time, it urges students to find win-win solutions to the case problems at the end of each chapter.

Research in composition over the past thirty years is the foundation of this book's writing philosophy. Such research strongly suggests that students mainly improve their writing in two ways: (1) by reading texts of the kind they will write, and (2) by writing them. Initial instructions and advice can be helpful, as can instructor commentary on work in progress. But the reading and writing are crucial. To provide practice in reading, *The Portable Business Writer* presents forty model business documents—most with commentary in the margin—and asks students to study additional documents found outside the textbook. To provide practice in writing, each chapter offers a selection of carefully constructed assignments, mostly case studies that give depth and authenticity to the writing context.

Design, Features, and Use

Chapters in *The Portable Business Writer* open with instructional text that focuses on specific, practical strategies for writing the beginning, middle, and end of the type of document under discussion. The instructional text is concise; and the content uncluttered by anecdotes, sidebars, photos, cartoons, and other nonessential filler. One or more model documents follow. An extensive set of problems for class work and homework concludes the chapters.

One way instructors can use *The Portable Business Writer* is to follow this classroom-tested pattern. It begins with students, individually or in groups, working out solutions to one or more problems in class. Then the instructor selects a method for reviewing that work, perhaps putting a piece of student writing on the chalkboard, checking the beginning, middle, and end against the advice given at the beginning of the chapter. Finally, the instructor selects another case problem for a formal, out-of-class writing assignment.

Students can use *The Portable Business Writer* to learn conventions that allow professionals to write quickly without reinventing solutions that are common property in organizations. But as they work on the case problems, students will also have the opportunity to take into account the complexity of human relations, and to learn that business writing is necessarily creative writing.

Acknowledgments

I wish to express my gratitude to my wife, Yoshiko, who supported me in every way and who provided invaluable expertise on Japanese business practices. I also wish to thank my editors at Houghton Mifflin: Terri Teleen, Janet Edmonds, Helen Bronk, and Karen Keady. I also wish to recognize the contribution of my father, Robert G. Murdick, author of numerous business textbooks, for his advice on business research and other topics.

Colleagues who reviewed early drafts of the manuscript helped develop its raw potential into a polished book. My thanks to:

Don Andrews	Chattanooga State Technical Community College
Arlene Bowen	Massachusetts Maritime Academy
Doug Desrud	
David L. Dyrud	Oregon Institute of Technology
Dan Jones	University of Central Florida
Pamela H. Lawrence	University of Massachusetts at Amherst
Jo Lundy	Southern Polytechnic University
William Pierce	Prince Georges Community College
Ronald E. Smith	University of North Alabama
Bill M. Stiffler	Hartford Community College
Hugh Stilley	GMI Engineering and Management Institute
Daphne Swabey	Eastern Michigan University
Janice Tovey	East Carolina University

Finally, I must toss a biscuit to Delmore, my Chocolate Lab, who sat under the desk as I wrote. His weight against my leg lightened the burden of authorship in a way that every dog lover understands.

W. M.

1

Making the Grade in Business Writing

Business writing courses tend to reflect the values of the workplace. Whereas a course in creative writing might encourage experimentation with language and the shape of texts, a business writing course emphasizes clear, unadorned phrasing and conventional formats, because that is what makes the most effective communication between people who work in organizations. This chapter discusses the general characteristics of business writing and offers advice on doing well in a business writing course.

1.1 Characteristics of Effective Business Documents

The following list of characteristics provides a check list for revising and editing your business documents. In general, effective business documents

a. Follow conventional formats that place important information, such as a date or return address, in predictable positions on the page where readers expect to find them
b. Are well laid out and perfectly neat
c. Are free of proofreading errors (for example, writing *teh* for *the*; leaving out or repeating words or letters)
d. Are free of grammatical errors and unconventional punctuation
e. Use a quiet, friendly, rational tone
f. Use a clear, natural style
g. Find creative ways to take into account the reader's needs while pursuing the writer's goals.

1.2 Planning and Revising

Writers of essays and scholarly articles frequently use a revision-heavy writing process. They sometimes plunge right into their writing without any significant planning and then look for "the line of argument" that emerges (Sommers, 1980, p. 384). These writers revisit their texts repeatedly, reading and revising, slowly building toward a finished product.

In the business world, writers do not always have the luxury of endless revising. Letters must get out; memos must be put into the paper flow so that work can get done. For this reason, writers of business communications often use a planning-heavy writing process, which allows them to complete the writing more quickly. They take enough time to figure out what should go into their letter or memo, they write it quickly, and then edit for phrasing and correctness.

As a student, you will probably have deadlines for writing assignments, but rarely, if ever, will you be asked to produce a finished letter or memo in one day. You will usually have several days at least to complete a writing assignment, if not longer. Because you have the time, you should use a revision-heavy writing process, which will help you develop better texts; but you should also use a planning-heavy writing process, which is how you are likely to produce short documents in the workplace, and which will help you get on the right track faster. In other words, do both: plan extensively and revise extensively.

1.3 Writing Effective Sentences

Beginning with your first draft, try to use your natural voice—the tone and language you would use when conversing with a favorite aunt, for example. Avoid the extremes of slangy informality and ponderous stuffiness.

The word processor can help you with neatness. If your document has even a tiny error, fix that flaw and reprint. Use the spell-check function, not only after the first draft is complete, but also after every subsequent revision or editing session. Get others to proofread your documents. Much work in modern organizations is collaborative. Asking someone to read and comment on a letter or memo you just wrote is not considered "cheating" in the workplace. Your business writing instructor may want you to get in the habit of getting help from others and, of course, returning the favor when others come to you with their texts.

Because college is a time of intense language growth, most students can expect to struggle with the problem of sentence-level correctness throughout their college years. This text provides lessons on common errors that show up in the writing of undergraduate students. Studying these lessons and checking your papers for these problems will eliminate some of your sentence-level problems. As an aid to that effort, you may wish to keep an error notebook in which you record the sentence-level problems that show up in each of your writings. You can use this notebook to identify the mistakes you repeat and to become more conscious of what to look for when you edit your texts.

English handbooks, such as *Keys for Writers,* 2nd ed., by Ann Raimes (Houghton Mifflin), provide another resource for learning to write correctly.

Most colleges and universities have writing centers that offer help at every stage of the writing process, including editing. In a workshop classroom, classmates may critique each other's writings.

Problems for Classwork and Homework

P1.1 Freshman Composition

Discuss the characteristics of writing that were considered important by your freshman composition instructor(s). How did those characteristics match, or differ from, the characteristics valued in business writing?

P1.2 Memos vs. Letters

Discuss differences between business memos and letters. (a) Are these forms used for different audiences? (b) Under what circumstances would each form serve multiple audiences? (c) Do they require or permit different levels of formality? (d) Can you imagine one purpose in writing for which you would always use a memo instead of a letter and one purpose for which you would always write a letter?

P1.3 Your Business Letters

Consider several business letters you have written. How did your method of writing those letters compare to the method recommended in this chapter for getting a good grade in this course?

P1.4 Study of Writing

In recent decades a great deal of research has focused on the nature of writing in the professional workplace. The following assignments ask you to explore that research.

a. In 1982 researchers Lester Faighley and Thomas P. Miller carried out a study of writing on the job. Read Faighley and Miller's report (*College English,* 44.6, Oct. 1982, 557–569) and write a summary of their findings.
b. Read and write a summary of Paul V. Anderson's "What Survey Research Tells Us about Writing at Work" in *Writing in Nonacademic Settings*, ed. Lee Odell and Dixie Goswami, Guilford Press, 1985.
c. Read and write a summary of James Paradis et al., "Writing at Exxon ITD: Notes on the Writing Environment of an R&D Organization," in

Writing in Nonacademic Settings, ed. Lee Odell and Dixie Goswami, Guilford Press, 1985.

P1.5 Interview Business Person

Talk to someone you know employed in a professional workplace. Find out how much and what kinds of writing this person does. Ask about the person's writing process. Try to obtain a sample of the person's writing to add to a short report on your findings.

2

Letter Format

This chapter describes formats for traditional business letters. Boxes 2.1 and 2.2 show options for formatting personal business letters written from your home. Boxes 2.4 and 2.5 show the formats recommended by the American Management Association (AMA) for letters written from the workplace using letterhead stationery.

Box 2.3 provides an example of a contemporary, "personal" style which ignores some of the traditions. However, it is best to master the conventional forms before creatively breaking the rules. Your business writing instructor may insist that you use only traditional formats for writing assignments.

2.1 Letterhead/No Letterhead

Business letters emanating from companies or organizations typically use letterhead stationery. The company or organization's name, address, phone number, and possibly other information are printed at the top of the page in an attractive style and layout.

Use letterhead stationery only for the first page of a business letter. Use regular paper for any additional pages, numbering those pages at the top.

When you write letters at home to solve your personal business problems, you would not normally use letterhead stationery.

2.2 The Heading

The heading of a letter with no letterhead includes your return address, but not your name. It also includes the date, the reader's name and address, and a salutation (Dear Mr. Wilton:). The arrangements are illustrated in the boxes.

When using letterhead stationery, the letterhead includes your return address, so you don't need to restate your address at the top of your letter (see Boxes 2.4 and 2.5).

The Re: line comes between the reader's address and the salutation. It briefly states the subject matter of the letter. It is optional, unless you are following strict AMA guidelines for letterhead business letters.

Box 2.1

Traditional Business Letter Format
Personal Letter/No Letterhead/Block Style

The letter begins with the writer's return address. (The writer's name does not appear in this section.)

Date

Blank line between sections

Reader's title and name

Reader's address

Blank line between sections

Salutation

Blank line between sections

First paragraph of the body

Blank line between sections

Blank line between sections

Closing

4–5 blank lines for a signature

Writer's name typed

Postscript

Mu Gamma Mu Sorority
645 Loeffler Boulevard
Youngsville, PA 15417
July 8, 19__

Mrs. Jeanine Wright
645 Bridge Street
Youngsville, PA 15417

Dear Mrs. Wright:

This is your daughter showing off her new ability to write formal business letters, thanks to her Intro to Business Writing course. Another reason I'm writing is to ask for a small increase in this month's allowance, say $40.00, so that I can take advantage of a special sale at the campus bookstore—a complete, beautifully bound, ten-volume collection of great literature for $39.95!

OK, the truth. Caroline and Bridge are going to dinner in Pittsburgh at a new rock-cafe-style dance place, and they're begging me to come with them. They want me to be the designated driver, which I don't mind. I can't let them down! (And without the forty I can't afford it.) You *do* understand, because you *were* a college girl once yourself!

Best regards,

Marilynn Wright

Marilynn Wright

PS: How do you like this letter form? See what a good student I am. Academic accomplishment should be rewarded, I always say. Love, Mari.

Box 2.2

Traditional Business Letter Format
Personal Letter/No Letterhead/Indented Style

Date and return address are set off to the right.

July 8, 19__

645 Loeffler Boulevard
Youngsville, PA 15417

Ms. Jane Chapman
Youngsville Elementary School
645 Bridge Street
Youngsville, PA 15417

Dear Ms. Chapman:

Paragraphs are indented.

My daughter Kelly will be in your 6th grade class next year. Kelly is a slow reader, but she is improving. Would it be possible for me to get copies of the textbooks you will be using for this class so that I can help Kelly get a head start with the reading?

I did this last year quite successfully, and Kelly's grades improved. I think that with one more year of preparation, Kelly will be reading at the same level as other children her age.

Thank you for any help you can give me for this project.

Sincerely,

The closing is aligned with the return address and date.

Melissa Angstrom

Melissa Angstrom

Box 2.3

A Contemporary Business Letter Format
Personal Letter/Personal Style

The writer decided to center the date.

Putting 4–5 spaces between the date and the return address is now common.

The writer decided to set the return address off to the far right side.

The writer decided to center and boldface the RE: line.

No salutation for unknown reader.

Polite but informal sign-off.

Extra blank lines between text and closing help this short letter fill the page.

The writer omitted the first line of the closing. Contemporary styles sometimes ignore conventions that are pure formalities.

April 9, 19__

668 Bolin Street
Carbondale, PA 15417

The Bath Shop
Carbondale Road Mall
Carbondale, PA 15417

RE: A request to stock Aloe Elixir Body Soap

I once found a product called Aloe Elixir Body Soap in a bath shop in L. A., and it was fantastic! I searched your store, but couldn't find it. The clerk who waited on me said that she'd never heard of Aloe Elixir.

Would it be possible for you to try to find that product in your ordering catalogues and order some for your store? If you're successful, please give me a call at 785-5555 and leave a message on my machine, or e-mail me at *ltownsend@zipp.net*. If you find this soap for me, you'll have a new regular customer.

Thanks.

Larry Townsend

Larry Townsend

Box 2.4

Traditional Business Letter Format Letterhead/AMA Block Style

Letterhead with enlarged name of organization, address, and phone number

KENT GORDON ELEMENTARY SCHOOL

645 Bridge Street, Youngsville, PA 15417
(412) 786-4037

Date is placed two lines above the target address.

October 8, 19__

Mr. J. J. Wilton
Assistant Fire Chief
Youngsville Fire Department
877 Clark Avenue
Youngsville, PA 15417

Re: (regarding) statement indicates the subject of the letter.

Re: Class picnic

Dear Mr. Wilton:

Our sixth grade students and I wish to thank you for the wonderful demonstration you and your firefighters provided us last Saturday. It was both educational and exciting. The students loved it, and they learned some important things about how to prevent and put out fires around the house.

At the end of each school year, we have a class picnic and we like to invite not only parents, but also other adults who have contributed to making our school year productive. I hope that you and the other firefighters who helped with the demonstration will be able to come. Your spouses and children are also welcome.

Our picnic will be at the Youngsville Community Park on May 22, from noon to five. Hope to see you there.

Sincerely,

Laura Jaymore

Laura Jaymore
Principal

chm

Box 2.5

Traditional Business Letter Format
Letterhead/AMA Modified Block Style

AMERICAN TESTING SERVICE
7622 Market Street, New York, NY
PH (555) 765-9005 FAX (555) 765-9006

The date is indented toward the middle.

March 5, 19__

Dr. Marcus Dunlevey
Associate Dean of Liberal Arts
Pumpkinville College
Pumpkinville, OH 44102

Re: Self-evaluation

Dear Dr. Dunlevey:

From your description of the sophisticated self-evaluation process that you have initiated at Pumpkinville College, I believe that our Collegiate Multilevel Self-Evaluation Attitude Survey (CMSAS) would be an appropriate tool for exploring the issues you mentioned in your letter.

This nationally norm-tested instrument would also significantly enhance the credibility of your self-study, while providing a picture of where Pumpkinville stands in relation to other colleges of similar size and character.

An ATS representative can come to your campus and demonstrate the product to you and your colleagues. Call or fax me if you have any questions or if you would like to make arrangements for a campus demonstration.

The closing is indented and aligned with the date.

Sincerely,

Ginger Martinio

Ginger Martinio

slb

Separate all sections of the heading with blank lines. As a general rule single blank lines separate sections in business letters.

2.3 The Salutation

This is the greeting, beginning with the word *Dear.* If you know the name of the person you are writing to, put in that person's last name (unless you and the reader are on a first-name basis). Often, when writing to companies, you don't know the name of the person your letter will go to. You should make every effort to find out that name, even if it means calling up the company on the phone and asking for the name of the "executive in charge of purchasing widgets."

If you cannot find out the reader's name, you can often identify the person by title (Dear Marketing Representative:). Or, if writing to someone in your own profession, you can refer to him or her as a colleague (Dear Colleague:). Otherwise, leave out the salutation altogether and, if you wish, give the Re: line more prominence (see the boldfaced, centered Re: line in Box 2.3).

2.4 The Body

The body is the part of the letter containing the text, the message. Put a blank line above and below each paragraph in the body. In the case of business letters that run close to a page in length, your text will be easier to read if you break it up into three to four lean paragraphs, rather than one or two thick ones.

2.5 The Closing

The closing is a formal statement of who sent the letter. It begins with a polite conventional expression such as *Yours truly, Sincerely yours, Sincerely, Best regards,* or *Respectfully,* followed by a comma. If using two words, capitalize only the first word.

After the opening expression, leave four or five blank lines for your signature, then type your name. If you have a formal title, put it below your name, as in the example in Box 2.4. Laura Jaymore (in Box 2.4) would use her title at work, when writing as a representative of the school, but not when sending a letter from home dealing with personal business.

2.6 Typist's and Writer's Initials

If someone besides the writer types the letter or memo, such as a secretary or someone in a typing pool, the typist puts his or her initials in the left column two blank lines below the closing. The initials always appear in lowercase letters. For example, if the typist's name were Pat Hanson Mitchell, the initial *phm* would appear (see Box 2.4).

If the letter is signed by someone other than the person who composed it, or if the signature space contains the company name, the writer's initials appear first in capital letters, the typist's second in lowercase letters:

Sincerely,

AMERICAN HOUSE PAINTERS

LW/phm

You should always make a copy for your own files of every letter you write. When working for an organization, that copy goes into your office file cabinet, and the initials constitute a record of who was involved with the communication.

2.7 Copies To

Copies of a letter may be sent to people other than the primary reader. If so, indicate who gets copies of the letter by typing *c.c.* or *Copies to* followed by the names. For example:

phm

c.c. Marvin Stipple, Laura Mason, Lewis Urdang

2.8 Enclosures

If additional documents are enclosed with your letter, indicate that by typing *Enclosure* (for one document) or *Enclosures* (for more than one) in the left column below any typist's initials or "copies to" information:

phm

Enclosure

2.9 Post Script

If you wish to emphasize a point by repeating it, or add an afterthought, or add a point on a subject other than the one directly covered by the letter, you can do so by typing *PS:* at the bottom of the letter, followed by a sentence or two.

> PS: I do hope you can make it to the conference next week. I need your advice on several matters.

2.10 Page Numbering

Number the pages of any letter that runs longer than one page, starting with the second page. Place page numbers at the top, flush left. Include the name of the reader and the date, as well as the page number. You might also include the total number of pages, especially if the letter runs more than two pages:

> Maxwell Jones
January 23, 1996
Page 2 of 3

Problems for Classwork and Homework

P2.1 Eliminate Flaws

Examine the letter below and list all the flaws in format. Use line numbers to locate where problems occur.

1 James Franklin
2 The Pepper Shop
3 101 Broadway
4 New York, NY 29034
5
6 Susan Monar
7 569 Levitt Street
8 Tuba City, AZ 52867
9
10
11
12 Dear Mr. Franklin,
13 First paragraph. First paragraph. First paragraph. First paragraph. First

paragraph. First paragraph. First paragraph. First paragraph. First paragraph. First paragraph. First paragraph. First paragraph. First paragraph.

Second paragraph. Second paragraph. Second paragraph. Second paragraph. Second paragraph. Second paragraph. Second paragraph. Second paragraph. Second paragraph. Second paragraph. Second paragraph. Second paragraph. Second paragraph. Second paragraph.

Sincerely

Susan Monar

P2.2 Two-Page Letter

Demonstrate your understanding of modern letter format by writing a two-page letter in which you describe to your instructor your relevant background for this course: your grade level and major in college, your work history, your familiarity with computers, your writing experience (especially business documents). Be sure to number the second page.

P2.3 Letter Variation

Analyze the form of an actual business letter. Use a letter sent to you, or obtain one sent to a relative or friend. (Your instructor may have left one or more samples on reserve in the school library for you to use, if you cannot find a letter elsewhere.) Indicate each place where the letter conforms to the AMA standards described in this chapter (Boxes 2.4 and 2.5) and each place where it deviates from those standards. Turn in a copy of the letter you are describing along with your analysis.

P2.4 Expert Advice

Show a secretary, or a professional who writes business letters, the model business letters in this text and ask this person how his or her preferred letter format differs from these models. Prepare a short written report in the form of a business letter to your instructor.

Memo Format

Memos are internal documents. They range from informal notes to formal reports. This chapter looks at the formatting of brief memos. Part 3 of this book describes how memo reports are formatted and organized.

3.1 Basic Format

The American Management Association (AMA) recommends that brief memos follow the form depicted in Box 3.1. The model in Box 3.2 shows a slight variation. Take a moment to examine those models.

Notice that the heading is double spaced. Use short paragraphs and put a blank line between them, just as you would for a business letter.

As the models show, memos typically do not use closings. They generally end with the last sentence, unless an immediate response is required. In the latter case, the memo would end with a term such as *Comment:* or *Response:* at the bottom with space for the reader to respond (see Box 3.2). The same memo would then be returned to the original writer. If you are responding to such a memo, make a photocopy for your files of the whole memo with your handwritten response included.

3.2 Re: Line

People search for memos in their files by looking at Re: (regarding) lines (also called "subject lines"), so the Re: line is often set off with lines drawn above and below, or by separating it from the rest of the heading with an extra blank line, or by putting it in boldface type or uppercase lettering. The Re: line should contain sufficient information that a person searching for the memo months or even years later will be able to recognize the correct memo from the information there.

3.3 In-Text Salutation

Although memos don't have formal salutations, writers occasionally begin the first paragraph by repeating the reader's name, followed by a comma:

Box 3.1

AMA-Style Memo Format

The heading is double spaced. Note that the writer has initialed her name.

To: Jesse Devou, Production Manager

From: Wendy Scott WS

Date: March 30, 1996

Re: The practicality of Wm. Marshall's proposal for a 5-sided tent

The body has the same form as a business letter: single-spaced paragraphs separated by blank lines.

Jesse, I assume that by now you have had a chance to study Marshall's provocative proposal that we develop a 5-sided tent. Both the executives and the marketing people really like the idea. Now we need to know from your point of view--is it doable? How costly will it be?

Because memos are internal documents, the style is often slightly less formal than that of a business letter.

I'd like to see a preliminary feasibility report by next Monday, if that's possible. We're going to discuss the Marshall tent idea at a Tuesday morning meeting. I'd like to study your response and maybe discuss it with you before that meeting.

Thanks.

Box 3.2

Emphasized Subject Line and Comment Line

To: Jesse Devou, Production Manager

From: Wendy Scott WS

Date: March 30, 1996

Subject: The practicality of Wm. Marshall's proposal for a 5-sided tent

---

I assume that by now you have had a chance to study Marshall's provocative proposal that we develop a 5-sided tent. Both the executives and the marketing people really like the idea. Now we need to know from your point of view--is it doable? How costly will it be?

I'd like to see a preliminary feasibility report by next Monday, if that's possible. We're going to discuss the Marshall tent idea at a Tuesday morning meeting. I'd like to study your response and maybe discuss it with you before that meeting.

COMMENT:

Mr. Jones, I was impressed by your report.

Or, if informality is appropriate:

Fred, I was impressed by your report.

3.4 Page Numbering

Use the same principles for memos as for letters. On memos, writers sometimes also repeat the Re: line after the reader's name, possibly in a shortened form:

Louis Widdenburg
Problems with Arcott Co. purchase
June 4, 1996
Page 2

3.5 Writer's Initials on Memos

Memo writers sometimes initial or even sign their name in the heading where their name has been typed, to verify that this memo came from them.

3.6 Copies To

If copies of a memo will be sent to people other than the main recipient, indicate that by putting a Copies To: line in the heading after the To: line, and then list the names. For example:

To: Pete Waters
Copies To: Marvin Stipple, Laura Mason, Lewis Urdang

If all the readers of this memo are of equal status, list them after the TO: prompt with a comma separating the names:

To: Pete Waters, Marvin Stipple, Laura Mason, Lewis Urdang

If sending the memo to a group, avoid listing names by using the group name:

To: Marketing Personnel

Problems for Classwork and Homework

P3.1 Eliminate Flaws

Examine the memo below and list all the flaws in format. Use the line numbers to locate where problems occur.

From: Jennifer Crisson

To: Max Harmon

Re: Report
2/16/96

Dear Max,

I'm glad to see that you finally finished the first draft of that sales report. Dennis should be satisfied with it. I certainly am, though I wouldn't mind a longer section on Boston. It looks like the Boston office will be the company leader this year. That's a surprise, given all the trouble they had at the beginning of the season. Do you have any theories as to why they were able to turn things around? Was it anything management up there did, or was it the result of local circumstances? That's the sort of thing we need to know if you are to learn anything from the Boston experience.

Sincerely,

Jennifer Crisson

P3.2 Actual Memo

Analyze the form of an actual business memo. If you have trouble finding one, your instructor may have left some on reserve in the library. Or you may be able to obtain one from an administrative office at your school. Write a memo indicating each place where the example memo conforms to the AMA standards described in this chapter and each place where it deviates from those standards. Turn in a photocopy of the memo you are describing along with your analysis.

P3.3 Expert Advice

Show a secretary, or a professional who writes memos, the model memo in this text and ask this person how his or her preferred memo format differs from this model. Write a short memo stating each place where the person's preferences conform to the AMA standards described in this chapter and each place where they deviate from those standards.

P3.4 Job Well Done

Demonstrate your understanding of memo form by sending a congratulatory message to your assistant, Fritz Weller, on a job well done, with a copy going to the director of marketing, Marlene Mason. Invent a few details for a short two-paragraph text.

P3.5 Memo To Yourself

An employee in your company has gotten the flu and is unable to make an overnight trip to attend a conference one hundred miles away next Saturday (invent relevant details). Your boss has written you a memo asking if you can go in that employee's place. Write your boss's memo (to yourself), using Box 3.2 as a model. Then write your response, in pen, at the bottom of the memo.

Composing E-Mail Messages

Electronic mail, or "e-mail," is a message system available on computer networks. If your workplace has a local network, you and your coworkers can send and receive messages back and forth. If your computer is hooked into an Internet provider, you can communicate via e-mail with people all over the world. Messages you receive are automatically stored, and you can reread them, forward them to someone else, or print them at any time, until you decide to erase them. You can also store copies of your own messages on your computer or in allotted space on a mainframe or server.

Most local networks limit space for saving your own and others' messages. Some computer-systems managers erase e-mail files periodically. To prevent losing important messages you can print and file them as you would any other memo or transfer them from e-mail storage to your computer's hard disk (or to a floppy disk), where you can later access them using your word-processing software. When you first enter a new e-mail environment, find out how the local system works.

E-mail's great advantage for short, routine messages is its speed—office mail usually arrives a day after it is sent—and that it eliminates the problem of telephone tag. Sally Jones may be out of the office every time you call on the phone, and you may be out of the office every time she calls back, but you and she can communicate via e-mail without being in your offices at the same time.

4.1 Technical Limitations

In order to send your e-mail text over wires, your computer formats the text in ASCII (American Standard Code for Information Interchange; pronounced AS´ KEY).

ASCII, unlike the "rich" text used in word processing, does not process font modifications such as underlining. The conventional way to indicate underlining in e-mail messages is to put the underline character before and after:

```
Weber's book, _The Marketing Mind_, was helpful.
```

4.2 E-Mail Style

The instantaneous nature of e-mail transmission allows office workers to carry on informal discussions of work issues throughout the day, sometimes in rapid repartee fashion. This conversational character has led to a tradition of informality in the case of short, routine electronic messages:

> Sure, I can meet at 1:00 today to discuss the newsletter.
> Where? How about East conference Room

The above message lacks both salutation and sign off. It provides minimum explicit context, because it is part of an ongoing conversation and the previous message or messages provide the full context. The writer uses sentence fragments, drops the article in front of East, doesn't bother to correct the inconsistent capitalization in "East conference Room," and omits the question mark after the final interrogative.

Although that kind of informality is acceptable when the purpose of your short message is to quickly communicate one or two pieces of information, a long informal memo filled with uncorrected typographical errors would be a struggle to read.

Also, you should be sensitive to the tone conveyed by your routine messages. Messages like the one above can sound curt or impersonal. Merely adding a salutation would soften the tone:

> Bill,
> Sure, I can meet at 1:00 today to discuss the newsletter.

4.3 Providing Necessary Context

It is important to distinguish between the brief conversational e-mail message you send as a quick response and one in which you respond to a message sent a day or two ago. Suppose your colleague, Fred Adamson, on Friday afternoon sends you a reply to one of several e-mail messages you had sent him during the week, and you don't see his message until Monday morning. It reads

> Great idea. Let's do it.

In the worst scenario, you neglect to save a copy of your original message for yourself, Adamson can't remember what proposal of yours he was commenting on, and he erased your e-mail message after replying to it. The "great idea" is lost.

A message that may not be read for days, or that responds to a message sent days ago, should repeat information from the previous text(s) to create a full context. That means plan your message and then read over your first draft, making whatever revisions seem appropriate. Resist the impulse to dash down a phrase or two and click the SEND button.

To return to Adamson, instead of "Great idea. Let's do it," he should have written something like this:

> I really like your idea of offering Marlough a quarter share of the first year profits from the Allentown outlet, as a down payment on the building we'd be purchasing from him for that venture. Let's make the offer when we meet with him on Tuesday, Apr. 7, and see what he says.

Although providing a context is important, e-mail messages are usually short, and it is considered bad etiquette to ramble. Use a concise style. Keep paragraphs brief, with a blank line between them.

These generalizations don't preclude the use of e-mail to convey substantial documents. As a matter of convenience and speed, you may wish to send an important, two-page, tightly written text electronically, instead of through the in-house mailing system or via "snail mail" (the U.S. Postal Service). In such an instance, you should format the e-mail message just as you would a word-processed memo or report, with full headings.

Take time to plan, revise, and edit long formal messages so that your electronic text has the same professional look, clear and errorless phrasing, and coherent content that you would want in any of your important business documents. The progress report you e-mail to your immediate supervisor may get printed, distributed to higher-level executives, and discussed around a conference table. You don't want the most important people in your organization puzzling over a casual, sloppy, contextless report with your name on it.

4.4 The Privacy Issue

Some writers view their on-the-job e-mail messages as private, like phone calls or face-to-face conversations. They wouldn't expect management to tap their phone or bug their office, so they assume that no one will tap in on their e-mail communications or raid their computer e-mail files. Based on that assumption, an employee may say something jokingly nasty about "Old Bullet Head," the president of the company, in an e-mail message to a friend down the hall. That can be a terrible mistake. Many companies view on-the-job e-mail as company property, the same as memos and reports. Just as a manager wouldn't hesitate to delve into a central filing cabinet to find and read a memo you wrote last month, that manager might not hesitate to invade your computer files to read an e-mail memo.

It is best to be circumspect at all times and businesslike in all your on-the-job writings.

Problems for Classwork and Homework

P4.1 Tips and Tricks

Explore the e-mail system at your school. Bring to class some "tips and tricks" and be prepared to share them with your classmates.

P4.2 Analyze E-Mail Message

Obtain, with permission of the author, an e-mail message sent by an employee of your school or after-school workplace. (Your instructor may have left one or more such messages on reserve in your school library.) Analyze the message's level of formality, neatness and correctness, and fullness of context. Submit your analysis to your instructor in memo form, attaching a printed copy of the e-mail message.

P4.3 Message Clean Up

Tired at the end of a long day, you wrote the following sloppy, error-ridden, rambling e-mail message to your boss, Cynthia Marsh. Fortunately, you had the presence of mind to read it over and see the need for improvements before sending it. Write a revision.

> Well, Cyn, I hope this catches you before you leave the office today, otehrwise youll get it tomorrow. I had to pull Meyers off the fund raising thing, needed her help to get the sales letters out this afternnon. She was miffed, I think. Will you talk to her? By the way, I think shes' doing a good job with the fundaraising but that's charaity and we don't make aprofit there. Profit! That's the naem of the game, right? I need ber full time in my dept. Maybe next year we could get someone less effective to do the charity work. I don't mean less effective at charity, but. . . you get my drift. I'll think of someone. If you have any ideas on that, of courrse. Well, the clock's at 5:15 and my spouse is awaiting. Gotta go. Tommorrow!

P4.4 Newsletter Message

In the course of one afternoon, the following e-mail exchange took place between you and Jeff, a person you supervise at work:

YOU: Jeff, I'd like to change the format of our newsletter, and I'd like your input. I think that we need to put news stories first, starting on the front page, instead of having personal articles start there. What do you think?
JEFF: I agree. Get the news up front. Announcements too.
YOU: Perhaps we could have an Announcements page with its own heading.
JEFF: Sounds good.

The next week you decide to assign Jeff the job of completely redesigning the company newsletter. Your first draft of an e-mail message looks like this:

YOU: Jeff, I'd like you to take on the redesign job. Start with the ideas we talked about and then use your own judgment.

Revise your message to provide a sufficient context. Add any other information that you think would be helpful (for example, more on what you're looking for in a new design; a target date for a progress report or completion of the project).

P4.5 Privacy Policy

Your supervisor, Lonnie McDougal, has been asked to develop an e-mail privacy policy for your company. She has assigned you to do the research and provide her with information and arguments for a first draft. Although the top executives believe that the company has the right to monitor e-mail communications, she wants a policy that respects both the privacy rights of individuals and the rights of the company to have access to work done on the job. Research this issue. Locate and use published company policies as a source of ideas. Write a substantial, polished e-mail message to Lonnie McDougal presenting data useful for taking a compromise position. Identify your sources (see chapter 16 on documenting sources if you need guidance on avoiding plagiarism).

5

Planning Business Documents

Donald Murray, Pulitzer Prize–winning journalist and long-time writing teacher, says that "The most important writing usually takes place before there is writing" (1985, p. 17). Murray is referring to the thought and work that writers undertake in preparation for the first draft: mulling over the writing problem; talking with people; jotting down notes as ideas occur; researching; composing in the mind, perhaps on the way to work; making outlines. These activities are crucial parts of the writing process for most experienced writers. This chapter will help you develop a repertoire of formal planning techniques.

5.1 Analyzing Your Audience

The logical first step in planning is to consider your readers and their possible needs. For example, an audience outside your profession will usually need more information than an expert audience. At the outset of the planning stage, you may want to carry out a formal analysis of the audience by writing down relevant audience characteristics. The results of your analysis would affect decisions you make during all stages of writing: planning, drafting, revising, and editing. When you conduct a formal analysis of your audience, consider the following characteristics:

1. **Their knowledge of the subject.**
   How much will you have to explain?
2. **Their purpose in reading.**
   What do the readers need to know to do their job?
3. **Their predisposition toward the issues.**
   Are you addressing a group that agrees with your views or disagrees?
4. **Their personal characteristics.**
   What is your audience's age; gender; educational level; racial, ethnic, or regional identity?

5.2 Invention Techniques

After gathering information, you must "invent" much of your business text as you decide what to say and how to use the information. You may have the facts on your desk in the form of notes, but the ideas you need to fulfill your writing purpose will have to come out of your imagination.

Writing experts have devised a number of prewriting techniques to help writers get started generating ideas, including the following:

- **Listing**—quickly list every idea that occurs to you about your subject, in no particular order, just to get the thoughts out where they can be seen.
- **Brainstorming**—similar to listing but usually done in a group: individuals throw out ideas and someone writes them down.
- **Mapping**—place a focus word in the middle of a page and create branches leading out as ideas occur to you. Here's one for a letter of complaint about a bad paint job:

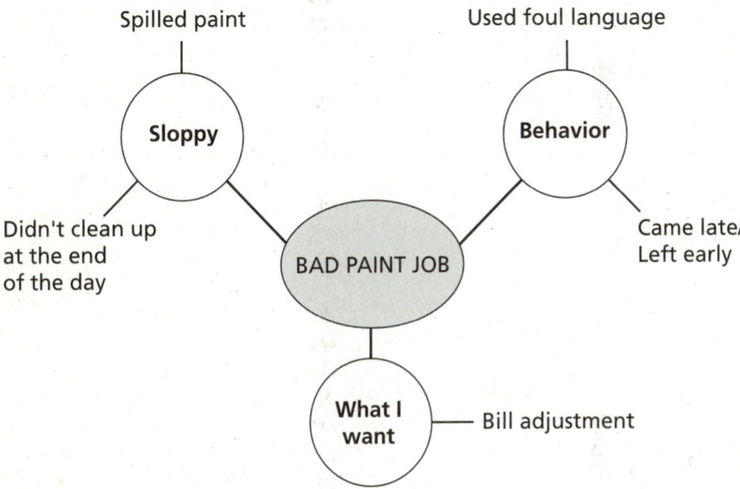

- **Journalist's WH-questions**—Answer who, what, when, where, why, and how about your subject.
- **Problem-solution**—Almost any writing task can be conceived of as a problem requiring a solution (Hoey, 1983). Generate ideas by answering these questions:
  — What problem am I trying to solve with this document?
  — What caused the problem?
  — What unsuccessful solutions have been tried or promoted?
  — What unsuccessful solutions might occur to the reader?

— Why do these solutions fail?
— What is my solution?
— Why will my solution work?

5.3 Organizing Ideas

After you generate some writing ideas, group them according to logical associations, a process called "clustering." For example, after listing ideas for a letter of complaint, put those that relate to background information in one group, those that relate to what went wrong in another, and those that relate to what you want in recompense in still another. The initial clusters are not immutable; change them as you write if you see a better way to group your information.

Some writers go a step further and create a semiformal or formal outline. Semiformal simply means that you use your own rough method of outlining, for example:

```
Bad Paint Job
The workers:
  1. They were sloppy
     —spilled paint on the parking lot
     —didn't clean up at the end of the day
  2. Their behavior was crude
     —no shirts
     —used foul language
What I want:
  1. a bill adjustment for the spilled paint
  2. an apology
```

For long documents, many writers use the most elaborate organizing device, the formal outline (see Box 5.1). The formal outline allows you to "see" the whole document, when the document is too long to hold in your conscious mind. The outline shows you what you have to do to complete the writing project, and as you write each part you'll have a sense of how it fits into the whole, which helps you to know what to say in each part.

5.4 Planning Letters

Although long reports may have complicated structures, the internal organization of a business letter is usually fairly simple. Think of letters as having three parts: an opening, a middle section, and a conclusion. Ask yourself first: How shall I orient my reader to me and to the main

Box 5.1

Types of Formal Outline

Traditional Outline

Recommendation to Buy Stock in Southern Bell

I. The Communications Industry
 A. Effects of deregulation
 B. Competition
  1. Cable TV
  2. The Internet
   a. Speed differences
    (1) Transmission speeds
    (2) Traffic capability
     (a) Expense
     (b) Wire vs. satellite
   b. Cost difference
II. The SBC Company
 A. Description of the company. . .

Decimal Outline

Recommendation to Buy Stock in Southern Bell

1.0 The Communications Industry
 1.1 Effects of deregulation
 1.2 Competition
  1.2.1 Cable TV
  1.2.2 The Internet
   1.2.2.1 Speed differences
    1.2.2.1.1 Transmission speeds
    1.2.2.1.2 Traffic capability
     1.2.2.1.2.1 Expense
     1.2.2.1.2.2 Wire vs. satellite
   1.2.2.2 Cost difference
2.0 The SBC Company
 2.1 Description of the company. . .

message? Then ask yourself: What information and lines of reasoning must I include in the middle of my letter to achieve my overall purpose? And finally: How should I close out this letter? What, if anything, must I ask the reader to do? How can I add a polite finish?

5.5 Planning Memos

Memos are often informal and short. They usually communicate routine messages between people who work closely with one another. The memo and letter assignments in this book, however, call for complex communications requiring a strategy. The three-part general strategy used for letters works equally well for memos.

5.6 Using Strategy Sheets for Letters and Memos

You may find it easier to plan your letters and memos if you create a strategy sheet like the one in Box 5.2. You develop a strategy—*what you're going to say*—and then put it in the boxes to the left. Then you write the actual sentences—*how you'll say it*—in the larger rectangles. When you're finished, you're ready to type up the first draft of your document.

Problems for Classwork and Homework

P5.1 Brainstorm

Form a group with several of your fellow students. Imagine that your high-volume carpet and tile wholesale company is searching for a new trucking firm to deliver orders to twelve retail outlets in a three-county area. You decide to write a letter of inquiry to send out to various local trucking firms asking about their availability, services, charges, and so on.

a. As a group, brainstorm and cluster ideas to develop a content for your letter to the trucking company's owners. (Invent details during your brainstorming.)
b. Individually, develop the clustered ideas into a rough outline.
c. Develop your rough outline into a strategy sheet for a three-part business letter.
d. Write the letter. Invent names and addresses. Design letterhead stationery.

P5.2 Formal Outline

Obtain a formal business report of at least four pages in length. Your instructor may have left sample reports on reserve in the school library.

Box 5.2

Using a Three-Part Strategy

Strategy	First Draft of the Text
Identify myself (account #) Statement of the problem	I am a US-TV subscriber, account number 567-920-89. My bill for July and August is $24.00 higher than usual. A copy is enclosed. I have not been notified of any raise in rates, so I assume there has been a billing error.
Include these details: My normal bill ($70) and the bill I received ($94) My request for a net-work channel Never received that channel	I subscribe to the basic package at a rate of $35.00 per month, and my bill for two months has always been $70.00. My bill for July and August is $94.00. I have a possible explanation for the $4.00. When I sent in my last payment for May and June, I requested the addition of a network channel at a rate of $2.00 per month. But because I have not yet received that channel, I shouldn't be billed for it.
What I want: —Review of my bill —Explanation of problem —Installation of network channel	Please review my bill and inform me of the outcome. Also, I would like to start receiving the network channel.

Or, if possible, obtain a copy of an actual report from a company or organization. Without reading the report, but by examining its major headings and subheadings, write a formal outline that captures the report's content.

P5.3 Analyze Letter

Obtain an actual business letter. If you haven't received one recently, borrow one from a relative or friend (be sensitive about privacy). Your instructor may have left one or more sample letters on reserve in the school library. Fill in a strategy sheet showing how the writer must have planned the letter. Write what you imagine was the strategy in the boxes to the left and the actual text in the rectangles to the right. Include a photocopy of the letter when you turn in the assignment or cut and paste sections of the letter into the right side of the strategy sheet.

P5.4 Analyze This Letter

In a letter to your instructor, describe the three-part organization of the following letter. Consider the Re: (regarding) line as the first significant part of the letter.

> PUMPKINVILLE SAVINGS & LOAN
>
> Sally Stover
> P.O. Box 56
> Pumpkinville, OH 15819
>
> Re: CUL Loan Disbursement
>
> Dear Ms. Stover:
>
> We have made the first disbursement of your CUL loan for the semester beginning August 27, 19__, to Pumpkinville College in the amount of $1,165.00.
>
> If you have any questions, please contact me at (412) 938-4444.

P5.5 Analyze Audience

Obtain an actual business letter or memo. Your instructor may have left samples on reserve in your library. Analyze the text in terms of what it reveals about the audience, at least the audience as conceived by the writer. Consider each of the four major concerns listed in section 5.1. Write a profile of the reader and send it in memo form to your instructor. Include a photocopy of the text you have analyzed.

P5.6 Dream Bathroom

You are building a new home and you've decided to splurge on a dream bathroom, complete with elaborate shower and tub with water jets. In a magazine you notice an advertisement for an unusual shower that appears, from the pictures, to have about fifteen massage jets squirting water from various angles. Just what you've been looking for! But certain questions arise in your mind regarding installation, water pressure, and cost. Plan a letter to the company, Nemo's Aqua Unlimited, requesting information.

a. Begin by filling in the left column boxes on a strategy sheet.
b. Complete your plan by drafting sentences into the boxes on the right side of the sheet.

6

Revising for Purpose and Audience

A planning-heavy writing process is useful for getting documents off the desk and into the paper flow in a timely fashion. Nevertheless, the more complex and difficult the writing task, the more revision must play a role. Professional writers rarely create a finished document the first time; it's even harder for a beginning writer to do so. When the message is important or sensitive, you may have to go through several "re-visionings" to achieve your purpose in regard to your audience.

6.1 Transforming Your Text

Prose writing can be classified into three distinct types: expressive, transactional, and poetic (Britton et al., 1975). Poetic writing, which is writing done for the enjoyment of language, is usually inappropriate in business writing, except perhaps for advertising and promotional material. Consider this anecdote from Ed Norwood, a former executive for U. S. Steel. Norwood recalls a district manager who used to sprinkle his reports with witty quotations from Shakespeare, Byron, and other classic poets. Norwood's comment: "We all loved reading his reports. But he never got promoted."

Expressive writing, as defined by Britton et al., refers to prose that writers use to develop thought, to get ideas and feelings out in the open where they can be contemplated. Expressive writing is usually intended for the author's use and no one else's.

Transactional prose serves a practical purpose: it conveys information, ideas, and persuasive arguments to other people. Business writing clearly falls into this category. But writers often begin complex writing tasks with expressive writing, creating a tentative first draft that no one might see but the author. A complex business text might begin with an expressive first draft that is transformed through revision and editing into transactional prose ready to be read by others.

Poor business writing sometimes looks like expressive prose, left as it first popped out of the writer's head. Technical-writing expert Linda

Flower (1979) calls that kind of text "writer-based prose," because it reflects the writer's discovery processes and interests and ignores the reader's needs. A text fully transformed through revision will reflect the writer's purpose *in relation to* an audience. (See Boxes 6.1–6.3.)

6.2 Understanding Purpose

Business writers can have a wide variety of purposes in creating their documents:

1. **Assign work.** Tell employees what to do
2. **Inform.** Provide readers with necessary information to make decisions and get work done
3. **Request.** Ask for favors or information
4. **Persuade.** Convince readers to take a particular course of action: to go ahead with a project or to make a particular purchase
5. **Document decisions.** Make a written record of who said what to whom, when, and where
6. **Report on work.** Show results of a study, indicate the status of a project, document the writer's contribution to a project
7. **Promote the company.** Project an attractive image for the organization. Sell goods and services
8. **Schmooze.** Maintain good relations. Fulfill social obligations

Writers often have multiple purposes. You must inform, for example, in order to sell. Persuasion figures into many purposes. Writers must juggle these purposes with decisions about content and at the same time consider the needs of the audience. Given this complexity, it is easy to lose sight of your purpose. Beginning writers sometimes produce texts that read well but work against what they are tying to achieve through the document. Imagine, for example, that you are trying to get the business next door to loan you a truck for a small job. This statement, while virtuous for its honesty, would probably be counterproductive:

```
I admit that I have no service I can offer you in return. . . .
```

A writer paying attention to purpose would probably leave out such a comment.

Beginning writers sometimes make the mistake of focusing strictly on the subject, saying everything about the subject that can be said, burying the point of the communication. In college, you get credit for parading your knowledge, but in the professional workplace, your writing will be valued for how efficiently it gets work done. That means focusing on your purpose.

6.3 Understanding Audience

The audience for a text, in the simplest terms, is the reader. In the traditional understanding of audience, the reader is a single real person (or group of people), known to the writer and possessing identifiable characteristics. As discussed in chapter 5, during the planning stage the writer might analyze the audience in terms of those features. Knowing your readers' level of knowledge of the subject, their purpose in reading, their predisposition toward the issues, and certain personal characteristics such as age and gender, will help you communicate with them.

The issue of audience begins to get complicated when we realize that a single document may have more than one type of audience. J. C. Mathes and Dwight Stevenson (1991) point out that business writers often have:

Primary Audiences: Those who will act on your message by making decisions.

Secondary Audiences: Those who will implement the decisions made.

Immediate and Nominal Audiences: Those who first receive your message for reasons of organizational structure or protocol and then pass it on to the primary and secondary audiences.

In addition, a document may address issues relevant to

- audiences in your own department
- audiences in related departments
- audiences distant in the organization
- audiences outside the organization (Mathes & Stevenson, 1991, pp. 42–47).

Different audiences may vary in their degree of knowledge of the subject, the kind of information needed to do their jobs, their predisposition toward the message, and their general educational level or other demographic characteristics.

In addition to the complexity of multiple audiences, modern theories of audience have raised questions about how well writers can actually know their audiences (Ede & Lundsford, 1984; Ede, 1984; Kroll, 1984; Kirsch & Roen, 1990). Business writers must sometimes address people they don't know personally. Furthermore, even the writer's understanding of a "known" audience actually consists of a "fictional version" of that audience in the writer's imagination. We can't know anyone's views perfectly, neither can we understand exactly what our readers know and don't know about a subject nor anticipate precisely what they will need to know to get their work done.

Writers also invoke a role for their audience to play, and then invite their readers to adopt that role and become that fictional audience. For example, if you were trying to persuade your company's president that the company should contribute to a charitable fund to protect the environment, you might begin your pitch this way:

> "As a community leader who appreciates the importance of a clean environment, not only for our business but for our society, you might wish to consider. . . ."

In this way, the writer invokes the sort of audience who would be attracted to the writer's cause.

Despite the complexity of audience, it is undeniable that good writers of transactional prose ponder the effects of their words on their imagined readers. This continual reflection is an important part of the writing process for competent writers (Ede, 1984).

6.4 Making the Tough Choices

In a study that compared the revision habits of college students with those of professional writers, Nancy Sommers (1980) found that the students tended to make changes on the word or sentence level, whereas the professionals often changed large chunks of their documents. The students mainly "scratched out" words and phrases, while the professionals added as much new text as they deleted. In other words, the beginning writers shied away from real revision; they merely edited their writings at the sentence level. The professionals remade their texts.

It is hard to admit that a beautiful paragraph—your favorite passage in the text—must be discarded because it doesn't serve your writing goal or address your audience's needs. No one likes to stare down at a first draft and realize that the whole approach is wrong. But you need that kind of tough-mindedness about your own prose to be an effective writer. Sometimes you have to do it wrong before you can figure out how to do it right. Revision is the process of seeing what's wrong and striking off in a new direction. It requires honesty. It takes courage.

Problems for Classwork and Homework

P6.1 Relevant Content

You and your best friend will be attending a college in Panama City, Florida. You decide to write a business letter to a large real estate agency in Panama City to request information about apartments. In preparation, you and your friend (who will be your roommate) brainstorm some ideas for the letter. You come up with the list below. Before clustering your ideas for content, you decide to revise your list. Keeping in mind your purpose for writing this letter, determine which of these ideas are relevant content and which are not. Defend your decisions.

a. Your interest in competitive tennis
b. Your financial circumstances
c. Your parents' names
d. You like listening to Elton John on your stereo.
e. Your roommate keeps a loaded gun in the bedroom for protection. You own a dog.
f. You have one car between you.
g. Your roommate's medical problems
h. You are both nonsmokers.
i. You are both vegetarians.
j. The kinds of houses you now live in
k. You own and regularly use an elaborate workout station.
l. Your roommate fears snakes.

P6.2 Analyze a Letter's Purpose

Examine an actual business letter to determine its purpose(s). Your instructor may have left some samples on reserve in your school's library. You might review the list of purposes in section 6.2. Submit your analysis in the form of a memo to your instructor. Quote passages to support your analysis. Attach a photocopy of the business letter you are describing.

P6.3 Analyze Memo's Purpose

Examine an actual business memo to determine its purpose(s). Your instructor may have left samples on reserve in your school's library. You might review the list of purposes in section 6.2. Quote passages to support your analysis. Submit your analysis in the form of a memo to your instructor. Attach a photocopy of the business memo you are describing.

P6.4 Critique Bad Letter

In the letter below, as a first step in the revision process, cross out statements that are irrelevant or that work counter to the writer's purpose.

> I am writing to ask for a recommendation. I have an opportunity to land a job with the Carlton Works as an assistant accountant. Carlton has been in business since 1938. It's an old and respected steel products manufacturer. I'll even have my own office, assuming I get the job.
>
> I'm sure you remember me. I took you for Cost Accounting last year. I got an A. In fact, my GPA is 3.9, and every professor I have asked for a recommendation has given me one.
>
> You may want to discuss my personal qualities as well as my academic strengths. I dress neatly and behave politely. I was on the wrestling team for two years, and I was treasurer of the student government.

As I said, I have a lot of recommendations and you may be thinking that yours isn't crucial, but because you are an accounting professor I feel your recommendation is important. Thank you.

P6.5 Shopping List

You just met your new roommate an hour ago, and he or she is going food shopping. You can't go along because of a prior engagement, so you need to write down a list of things for your roommate to pick up for you. Use this writing exercise as an opportunity to explore the idea of audience. First, make a list of twelve supermarket items as if you were the only reader, the sole audience (for example, *ice cream, coffee, tooth paste. . . .*) Switch audiences and write a second list as if your new roommate were the reader (*half gallon Breyers French vanilla ice cream. . . .*)

P6.6 Catamaran Sale

You work for the "Small Cat" division of Blue Water Boat Builders. Your department is responsible for the design, building, marketing, and sales of small catamarans (two-hulled boats of the kind often rented at beaches). Your main line is called Swamp Glider, which comes in thirteen-foot and sixteen-foot lengths. The thirteen-foot sailboat retails for $2,500 complete; the larger one for $4,900, or $5,600 for the racing version.

As sales director, you have been courting a potential customer for six months, the U.S. Coast & Lake Sailing School, a national chain and one of the biggest sailing schools in the country. Today you got news that your sales efforts have paid off. U.S. Coast & Lake wants the Swamp Glider for its small-cat line. They want a price for eight hundred of the thirteen-foot model and eight hundred of the sixteen-foot racing version. That would significantly increase your sales for the year. They also want assurance that your company can produce this many boats within nine months.

a. Write a memo to your company president, Harry Walsh, announcing and briefly discussing this deal. Your company will need to make a considerable capital investment to get production up to speed for such an order, and you must convince Walsh of the long-term value of making this commitment. This memo will be the first step in making your case.
b. Write a memo to your colleagues in your department announcing and discussing this deal. Your relations with this group are friendly, and your communications are informal in tone.
c. After you have finished the two memos, write a short analysis of them, pointing out differences in language and content that reflect the different purposes and audiences.

Box 6.1

Model Problem: Revision

As a first year psychology major at a large state university, you had a difficult time in Professor Denning's Introduction to Psychology class. Denning seemed to have negative feelings about your gender and often made disparaging remarks laced with cutting humor about you and other students of your gender. You asked some students of the opposite sex to see their exam papers and found that those students got higher scores on essay responses than you did, even when your content seemed about the same as theirs, at least in your judgment.

Unfortunately, Dr. Denning is the chair of the department. You do not want him/her for an enemy. You will be working in this department for the next four years, and you know of at least one required upper-level course that you will have to take from Denning. Nevertheless, you are angry about the treatment you received in this course (in which you got a C for a grade). In your mind, a psychology professor, of all people, should be above stereotyping. You believe that this professor constitutes a real weakness in the department from which you intend to learn the basics of your life's profession. Write a letter to Dr. Denning protesting your grade and the mental harassment you experienced in the class.

Note: Although you may write your solution from either gender's veiwpoint, the solutions to this problem will be written from the perspective of a female student. This will make Professor Denning a male.

The letter on the right is an example of "expressive prose" in the extreme. The writer is letting off steam—a good thing to do, as long as she eliminates the flashes of anger in her revision. She has not yet developed an effective approach to the writing problem, but her first draft does bring out some useful points.

The writer should not assume that her appeal is a waste of time—for it surely will be if she takes that attitude.

The information here about her comparison of essays should be retained in the final version.

Referring to the APA Manual is another good idea, though the tone has to be changed.

An appropriate ending.

Box 6.2

Expressive First Draft

Dear Professor Denning:

How would you like to have to listen to someone denigrating males for three hours a week, every week for four months? That's how you make female students feel in your classes. At least Intro to Psychology.

I would like to appeal my grade in this course. I received a C, but I think I deserve a B. I assume that you are going to reject my appeal, but the student handbook says that, as part of the grade appeal process, I have to go to you before I take my complaint to the dean, so that's what I'm doing.

You referred to females as "fundamentally emotionally unstable" on two occasions, and that was not the worst of your remarks. I feel that your tendency to stereotype women in a negative way has interfered with your judgment when it comes to evaluating our written work in the course. I compared my essay responses with those of several men in the class, and their essays didn't seem to say anything more or anything significantly different from what my essays said, yet they all got more points. Over the course of the semester and three exams, those point differences add up to a letter grade difference in my final average.

I have nothing against you personally, but I expect to be treated fairly. Doesn't our professional association take gender bias seriously? You should reread pages 50–60 in the *APA Manual.*

I am willing to meet with you to discuss this matter at a time of mutual convenience.

Box 6.3

Solution to Model Problem: Revision of Expressive Draft

In this revision, the letter has been restructured to fit its purpose. This is a letter asking for a grade appeal, and that is how it begins.

In the middle section the letter appropriately presents the details of the complaint—the reasons why the grade is wrong, in the opinion of the author. And finally there is an action statement at the end, asking for a meeting.

This version retains a professional tone. Although Denning may never *like* this student, because of the complaint, he probably won't despise her either. Her courtesy will earn her some respect. She wisely never mentions going over his head to the dean, because that would sound like a threat and might be counterproductive. This version remains consistently focused on the writer's purposes—to initiate and lay out a case for a successful grade appeal, and to make this professor aware of the effects of his "humor" on female students.

Dear Professor Denning:

I would like to appeal my grade in Introduction to Psychology. I received a C, but I think I deserved a B.

At the same time, I would like to bring up another matter, which I believe is connected to my grade problem. Throughout the semester, in class, you made a number of denigrating "witty" generalizations about females, referring to us, for example, as "fundamentally emotionally unstable." No doubt you were being humorous and didn't expect the students to take these remarks literally or seriously. But as you know, our professional organization warns that such humor can be intimidating or harassing (I'm thinking specifically of pages 50-60 in the *Publication Manual of the American Psychological Association*).

To be honest, Dr. Denning, because your remarks ridiculing females were so frequent, I got the impression that at some level you may indeed believe that females are not as sharp as males at the kind of work expected of students in a psychology course.

That attitude, however subtle, may account for the fact that you graded my essay exam answers lower than you did those of several males in the classroom, even though I couldn't see any significant difference in what they wrote and what I wrote. Those gentlemen have kindly allowed me to photocopy their essay answers and I would like you to read their answers along with mine, to see if you don't agree that mine are of the same quality.

I would like to meet with you soon to discuss this matter. As a new student in the program, I don't want to get off on the wrong foot, but I feel that I owe it to myself to follow the university process for grade appeal in this case.

I look forward to hearing from you to set up an appointment.

7

Revising for Tone and Style

Tone is the sound your writing makes. Your letter or memo might come across as angry, polite, amused, neutral, crazed, or rational. The tone expresses your state of mind, or at least your *apparent* state of mind. Just as you sometimes control your emotions and bite back harsh words, you sometimes need to control your tone when you write, giving the impression of calm reasonableness when you might not feel that way. (See Boxes 7.1 and 7.2 for an example of effective revision for tone.)

In business writing, style refers to sentence structure and word choice as they affect clarity.

In workplace communications, clarity is the quality valued above all others (Faighley & Miller, 1982). Therefore, you should cultivate a plain, natural style that gets your points across clearly.

7.1 Appropriate Tone for Business Communications

When you write business communications, you want to appear as a quiet, rational, polite, helpful, optimistic person seeking cooperation in regard to a matter of mutual interest. Those adjectives are important. Consider each one for a moment:

quiet
rational
polite
helpful
optimistic

The optimistic part of your tone comes from your assumption that your reader is a rational, intelligent person of good will. Although you might not believe that at all, your tone should indicate such an expectation. Always give your reader a chance to be reasonable and decent. You can adopt a cooler tone in later communications, if necessary, but always be polite and calm no matter what circumstances develop.

Box 7.1

Model Problem: Tone

You are a car dealer, and you just received this letter from an unhappy customer:

> Dear Manager:
>
> You may remember me. I bought this lousy used car from you two weeks ago. Yesterday it wouldn't start after work. The place was locked up and I was darn lucky I had my car phone so I could call my old lady and get a ride home. The thing wouldn't start. The starter must be broken. It just went tick tick tick when I turned the key. What a piece of junk!
>
> I want you to haul that lemon back to your place and either fix it or gimme my money back! Pronto!
>
> With no best regards,
>
> Jesse Harmond

Your company does not tow cars, but you know the name of a garage that does: Pete's Auto Service, PH 567-9087. Most likely the battery is dead, probably because of a drain from the car phone, which shouldn't be left plugged in when the car isn't being run.

The first draft of your response was written in a huff. It appears below. Revise it demonstrating the courtesy and patience recommended in this book. Put in an appropriate heading, salutation, and closing.

YOUR FIRST DRAFT:

> We don't sell lemons at Merrytown Motors. Let's get that clear right from the start. If there's something wrong with your car just two weeks after purchasing it from us, it is probably due to your actions.
>
> I doubt that the starter is broken. More likely, your battery is simply dead because you stupidly left your car phone plugged in continuously for two weeks. You should of checked that before writing your nasty letter. Try jump starting your automobile. If that doesn't work, call a service station and have them tow your car to our place and we'll fix it under warranty. We don't tow cars. Don't you belong to AAA? They'll pay for the towing if you do. Otherwise Pete's Auto Service will do it. They're in the book.

Box 7.2

Solution to Model Problem

Merrytown Motors
483 Markey Street
Merrytown, OH 45201
564-785-9800

October 25, 19__

Mr. Jesse Harmond
650 Green Street
Merrytown, OH 45201

Dear Mr. Harmond:

I regret that you are having trouble with the automobile you recently purchased from our dealership. Before we sell a used car, we inspect it thoroughly and it must meet our high standards, so it is very unusual for a customer to have a breakdown soon after purchase. Although we do not own a tow truck, I can offer some suggestions for dealing with your problem.

You are right about starters; they sometimes break. But the most likely cause of your problem is a dead battery. The battery was fine when you left our lot, so something must have drained it. You mentioned your car phone. Many people don't know that a car phone, if left plugged in continuously twenty-four hours a day, slowly draws power from the car battery in some vehicles.

The first thing you should do is try to jump start your car with a set of jumper cables. If jump starting doesn't work, then your car indeed needs to be repaired. You should have it towed in to our place so that we can fix it under warranty. If you belong to an automobile club, like the AAA, call them about the towing. Otherwise, you might try Pete's Auto Service, PH 567-9087. Of course, if we were at fault and there are any necessary towing fees, we will cover them.

Again, I'm sorry you're having trouble, and I hope that you are able to solve this problem with a simple jump start.

Sincerely,

These principles apply not only to correspondence going outside your organization but also to internal communications. When you deal with office staff or colleagues at work, a harsh tone is almost never necessary and it creates ill will. At the very least, it may reduce the employees' ability to concentrate on work for the rest of the day. At worst, employees who are seriously hurt by your words may deliberately under-perform or even try to sabotage efforts in the office.

7.2 Controlling Your Level of Formality

Your writing tone will vary in level of formality. A formal tone can convey displeasure if used with someone you know well. Suppose, for example, you have an assistant, Sarah Smith, a young woman you play tennis with and who comes to your house for big family dinners on weekends. The two of you call each other by your first names. Now, compare these two versions of the same message:

> INFORMAL
> Sarah, I really need that Patterson Hills report, which was due a month ago. Hey, this is the third reminder. Can't you drop everything and get it to me? Thanks.

> FORMAL
> Ms. Smith, you have not yet submitted your report on the Patterson Hills Project, even though it was due a month ago and I have reminded you twice since the due date. Please put aside your present activities and work on the Patterson report only, until it is finished. Thank you.

If Sarah Smith received the formal version she would probably conclude that you were quite angry with her.

A formal tone, however, can imply respect if your reader is an important person whom you do not know intimately, while an informal tone in such a case would be insulting. Suppose you are sending a report to the president of your company, Margaret Jones, whom you have never met. Imagine the effect of this "cover memo":

> Margaret, you're gonna love this report! Get ready for some *great* news on the Patterson Hills thing!

She might conclude that you are a nut case and call her secretary for your personnel file. In this case the appropriate tone is one of respectful formality:

> Ms. Jones, attached is the Patterson Hills Project report. As you will see, it presents good news for our company.

You should vary the level of formality according to your relationship to your reader and the seriousness of the subject matter.

7.3 Avoid a Stuffy Style

Most business communications call for a plain, direct style. Sometimes beginning writers, in trying to achieve the appropriate formality and dignity for a business letter or report, adopt an unnatural, bloated, stuffy style. This kind of prose can be difficult to read:

> On February 14, it was requested of me that I initiate a study of our competitor's product line prices, in comparison with ours, to determine if, in fact, their prices represent a superior bargain than ours for the customer.

The same thing can be said more briefly and clearly by using an unadorned, natural style:

> On February 14, Mr. Heller asked me to compare our competitor's prices with ours to see who gives the better bargain.

Eliminate stuffy wording by addressing three problems:

1. Avoid verbs that are nominalized (turned into nouns).
   Stuffy: made a request for Clear: requested
2. Choose the active voice over the passive voice.
   Passive: I was asked to report
   or
   I was asked to report by Pamela Jones.
   Active: Pamela Jones asked me to report . . .
3. Select common words over uncommon ones.
   Stuffy: An absence of implementation of the policy will render the policy emasculate.
   Clear: Unless it is enforced, the policy will be useless.

7.4 Use Active and Passive Voice Appropriately

The active voice places the performer of the action (called the "agent") in the subject position. In the sentence *Mary promoted John,* Mary is the agent and the grammatical subject. The passive voice places the receiver of an action in the subject position, as in the case of "John" in this sentence: *John was promoted by Mary.* Mary is still the agent, but no longer the grammatical subject. When using the passive voice, the writer can (and often does) drop the agent: *John was promoted.*

Unless you are carefully avoiding liability, do not use passive constructions to dodge responsibility. Write *Our packaging department made a mistake in your order* not *A mistake was made in your order.* Sometimes writers use the passive voice, with deleted agent, so often that the reader is left with the impression that many things are happening but no one is doing them. To avoid that, make active voice your default voice, the one you use unless you have a specific reason for using the passive.

Passive voice is particularly suited to some uses:

- To indicate what is generally true: *Real estate is valued for its location.*
- To state what usually happens: *Accounts are balanced monthly.*
- To achieve the desired focus. In the active voice *Teams carry out projects,* the emphasis is on what teams do. But if you wanted to focus on projects, you would use the passive: *Projects are carried out by teams.* The passive voice allows you to focus on the receiver of the action by placing it in the subject position.
- To ignore an unknown or irrelevant agent: *Most companies on this block were founded more than fifty years ago* instead of *Somebody founded most companies on this block more than fifty years ago.*
- To avoid a bragging tone in reports: *These goals were achieved by February* instead of *I achieved these goals by February.*

7.5 Emphasize Parallel Structure

You can increase clarity in complicated sentences by emphasizing the similar grammatical structure of elements in a list. You do that by repeating words that frame the elements. Consider the following sentence:

> This doesn't mean that you should never place material at the front of your sentences before the grammatical subject or never embed structures.

To make the sentence clearer we emphasize its parallel elements by repeating the phrase *that you should never*:

> This doesn't mean *that you should never* place material at the front of your sentences before the grammatical subject or *that you should never* embed structures.

7.6 Prefer Plain Language

Big words are impressive, but your first responsibility as a business writer is to communicate, not to show off. Technical language is indispensable in professional work, but it should be used only as necessary. Use ordinary language when possible, but don't confuse your reader by avoiding common, shared technical terms. If you write "the account added up," an accountant may wonder if you mean "balanced," and if so, why you don't say so.

Euphemisms are nice ways of saying uncomfortable things. The funeral director refers to your deceased relative as your "loved one," not your "dead uncle." Your tennis instructor, after watching your pathetically awkward serve, observes that your motion "needs some attention." But don't use euphemistic language to cover up embarrassing truths that you should face up to. If your company sent a customer a crushed lamp shade, don't refer to the delivered product as "imperfectly shaped upon arrival"—not unless you want to turn an upset customer into a furious one.

7.7 Cut the Fat

As you revise your text to create a more readable style, eliminate extra verbiage: unnecessary words (*circle around* instead of *circle*), wordy expressions (*at this point in time,* instead of *now*), and even full sentences or paragraphs that add nothing.

A trim style is easier to read than a bulky one. Richard Lanham (1992, pp. 3–4) makes an amusing game of reducing the "lard" from your prose. He asks you to revise and then figure out the "lard factor," the percentage of the original text that wasn't necessary. Here's his formula:

$$\frac{\text{Number of Words in the Original} - \text{Number of Words in the Revision}}{\text{Number of Words in the Original}} = \%\ \text{Lard}$$

Problems for Classwork and Homework

P7.1 Harmond's Letter

It is possible for a letter to be well structured and clearly written but offensive because of its tone.

a. Analyze Jesse Harmond's letter (Box 7.1) in terms of its three-part organization. Create a strategy sheet and write in the strategies in the left-hand boxes and enter the text (or photocopy, cut, and paste it) into the right-hand rectangles. Write a cover memo to your instructor evaluating the text from the standpoint of structure.

b. Rewrite Jesse Harmond's letter. Consider places in the letter where the language is too informal for a business communication as well as phrasing that shouts insultingly at the reader.

P7.2 Restaurant Policies

Employees in your restaurant are allowed one meal per shift from the lower-priced regular items (expensive specials are off limits). They are to eat their meal just before or just after their shift. It has come to your attention that many employees, from chefs to bus boys, are: (1) eating during work hours, (2) eating expensive specials, (3) pilfering hard-to-get spices and small quantities of other exotic foodstuffs for their cooking at home.

You decide to post a notice on the kitchen wall, and this is your first version:

Notice to All Employees

Let me remind you that employees are to eat before or after their shifts, not during. Anyone caught eating during a shift will be disciplined. And you are to eat the regular dishes, not the expensive specials. If I find that you have eaten a special, I'm going to deduct the cost from your pay check. If you keep on doing it, you may get fired.

I also know that some of you have been stealing spices and other foodstuffs from the kitchen. This must stop now. Anyone caught stealing from the restaurant will not only be fired but will be prosecuted to the fullest extent of the law.

I cannot understand how employees could abuse their positions and hurt their employer. It's like biting the hand that feeds you.

When you calmed down and thought about the situation, you realized that threatening your employees might undermine the quality of your kitchen and service. Firing one person makes everyone else nervous and glum and leaves you shorthanded until you can find a replacement.

Figure out reasons for your employees' undesirable actions. Then revise this notice in a manner that reflects your understanding of why the various violations of policy might be taking place, using a tone that will not alienate your employees. This will require you not only to change the threatening language being used, but also to come up with more creative solutions to the problems. Search for a way to give your employees what you think they want, without hurting the restaurant. For one or more of the problems, you may have to insist that the present policy be respected.

If so, explain why. But for the other problem(s), you should be able to think up changes in policy that will satisfy everyone. Remember: your employees are your team members, not your antagonists.

P7.3 Stuffy Style

Rewrite the following letter in a plainer style. Change any awkward or inappropriate passive-voice constructions to active voice.

> I wish to indicate my dissatisfaction with the upgrade performed on my computer by your company to the extent that, after the hard disk replacement, my communications program no longer works. No mistreatment of the disk was perpetrated at my headquarters.
>
> Whenever I attempt an Internet log-on procedure, the text suddenly proceeds to convert itself to gibberish characters. Every option on the Preferences menu has been experimentally altered, without the achievement of success.
>
> My hard disk is therefore being returned to you for your inspection and examination. If the program should be deemed unrepairable, please recompense me by including a new version of the software when you return my disk.

P7.4 Wordiness

Revise the passage below, eliminating unnecessary wordiness. Then compute the lard factor for the original text.

> TO: Dr. Jones, Ph.D.
> FROM: Sammy Wells
> DATE: September 18, 1999
> SUBJECT: My computer literacy and my record of work experience
>
> You asked me to write this memo in regard to my computer literacy and my experience with and knowledge of computerized devices. My experience with word processing with Word Perfect 4.0 is limited to my use of computers here at the university in the university labs. In other words, my knowledge of word processing is not an everyday occurrence due to the fact that I lack a home computer in my house.

You also asked me to describe the writing I do at work, where I am employed. I currently hold an assistant manager position at a local park near my home. My manager wanted me to compose and submit some grants for the park, to bring in money for projects, but I necessarily had to decline. In my opinion, I did not feel that I had the writing experience or ability to do that job. Therefore, my writing at work has consisted of the composing of short reports on my assigned projects.

P7.5 Readability Formulas

One controversial way of determining the readability of a text is to compute its Gunning-Mueller Fog Index, an analysis that assigns a grade-level to the text. A particular text assigned a sixth-grade readability level could presumably be read by the average sixth-grader.

a. Use your library to find the Gunning-Mueller Fog Index procedure. It appears in many published writings, including an insert in a *Wall Street Journal* article by William Blundell (August 28, 1980, Section 2, page 21). Analyze your most recent piece of writing for this course and report on its Fog Index grade level in a memo to your instructor,.
b. Read the Blundell article mentioned in a) above. The insert claims that the *Wall Street Journal* has a Fog Index of eleventh grade. Use the Fog Index procedure described in the insert to compute the grade level of Blundell's article. Report your findings in a memo to your instructor.
c. After looking at the Fog Index procedure, write a memo to your instructor discussing the value of such an analysis. Consider the factors that the Fog Index associates with sophistication and complexity. Would it be easy to write a text that had a low Fog Index but was quite sophisticated and difficult to understand? Or a text with a high Fog Index that even children might easily understand? Why, or why not?
d. Write a passage with a high Fog Index and then revise it to have a low Fog Index. In a memo to your instructor, present the two texts and an argument as to which, if either, is easier to read. Indicate whether both texts say exactly the same thing, or whether something was lost in the conversion.

Editing

When you have developed your business document until it seems effective, it is time to scrutinize the text at the word and sentence levels, looking for errors and moments of awkwardness. This is the editing process.

This chapter looks at the most common and the most distracting word-level and sentence-level writing errors that college students make. If you wish to study word and sentence conventions in detail, a traditional English handbook such as Ann Raimes' *Keys for Writers* (Houghton Mifflin) should serve your purpose.

8.1 Words Often Confused

Beginning writers often confuse homophones, distinct words that sound alike but are spelled differently: *minor* (adj. unimportant; n. underage person) and *miner* (person who works in a mine). You can develop memory tricks for homophones that give you trouble. For example, the word *mine* appears in *miner.*

These homophones arise frequently in business texts:

affect—The verb meaning "to change or cause to feel": The market drop will affect our profits.
effect—The noun meaning a result: The market drop will have an effect on our profits.
it's—The contraction meaning "it is": It's a good proposal.
its—The possessive pronoun meaning "belonging to it": I liked the report but not its title.
passed—The past tense of the verb *pass*: The market passed its former record high.
past—A noun or adjective meaning "time before now": He lives in the past even though his past life was uneventful.
personal—Adjective meaning "private" or "related to one individual": Her personal secretary . . .
personnel—Noun meaning "employees": He's in charge of training new personnel.

stationery—The paper you write on.
stationary—Standing still.
there—The locative adverb meaning "at that spot": The memo is there on the desk.
there—A meaningless filler in constructions with forms of the verb *be*: There are two reports due today.
their—The possessive pronoun meaning "belonging to them": It's their responsibility, not ours.
they're—The contraction meaning "they are": They're waiting for you in the conference room.
to—The preposition meaning "in the direction of": She went to the meeting.
to—The meaningless infinitive particle in constructions with verbs: She wanted to go.
too—The intensifier meaning "more than desired": The room was too hot.
too—Adverb meaning "also": We attended the meeting, too.

Besides homophones, several other related words are sometimes confused, in particular these:

between—Used to indicate the relationship between two items: It will be decided between the two of them.
among—Used to indicate relationships involving three or more: It will be decided among the three of them.
fewer—Used for countable items: fewer students, fewer dollars.
less—In formal writing, usually used only for mass items: less population, less money. Don't write less students.
number—Used for countable items: number of students, number of dollars.
amount—Used for mass items: large amount of wealth, the amount of sand. Don't write amount of dollars.
lie—To recline. I lie down every day / Yesterday I lay down / I have lain on this bed for days.
lay—To place. I lay the cat's food on the floor every day / Yesterday I laid the food on the floor / I have laid it on the floor every day for years.
principle—Rule of science, philosophy, or morality. His high principles kept him out of trouble.
principal—Main, most important; chief school administrator; the base amount: Early loan payments are mainly interest, affecting the principal only a little.
uninterested—Not interested.
disinterested—Usually used in formal writing to mean "neutral, having no personal interest." A judge should be disinterested in the case at hand, but not uninterested.

8.2 Possessives and Contractions

The possessive form is used for relations that imply "possession," as in *the boy's shoe,* but also for some relations that seem to have nothing to do with ownership, such as *last month's earnings*. Months don't literally own or possess anything.

Possessive constructions can be seen as an alternative way of expressing certain *of* constructions:

last month's earnings → The earnings of last month

When trying to determine if you should interpret a construction as a possessive (requiring an apostrophe), see if you can convert the structure to an *of* construction. If you can, you have written a possessive and you'll need an apostrophe.

Here are guidelines for spelling possessives:

1. Singular possessive: John's dog; the boy's shoe
2. Plural possessive: The two boys' shoes; three weeks' vacation (vacation of three weeks)
3. Plural possessive of words that have a plural form: the children's shoes; women's liberation
4. No apostrophe for possessives of personal pronouns: my; your; his; its; our; their. But other pronouns, such as *other,* take apostrophes just like nouns: each other's help; those others' help.
5. Contractions look like possessives: Fred's leaving means "Fred is leaving."

Note: An apostrophe is also used to form plurals of numbers, letters, and words: *He uses too many* too's *in his writing; her name has two* b's *in it.*

8.3 Run-Together Sentences

Run-together sentences are two or more sentences that have been attached without adequate punctuation:

You requested a memo on the closing here it is.
You requested a memo on the closing, here it is.

The two run-together sentences above can be corrected by using a period, a semicolon, or a comma with a coordinating conjunction:

You requested a memo on the closing. Here it is.
You requested a memo on the closing; here it is.
You requested a memo on the closing, and here it is.

Problems with run-together sentences often arise when beginning writers fail to distinguish between two kinds of sentence-connecting words, **coordinating conjunctions** *(and, but, or, nor, for, so and yet)*, which take commas in front of them when they connect two full sentences, and **transitional conjunctions** *(however, therefore, nevertheless, on the other hand, then)*, which require semicolons in front of them when connecting two full sentences. Thus, one correctly writes

The manager gave his approval**, but** you must work with Jack.

and

The manager gave his approval**; however**, you must work with Jack.

8.4 Agreement

Subjects and their verbs must agree in number. We write: *the manager believes* . . . and *the managers believe*. . . . We don't write *the manager believe* . . . or *the managers believes*. . . . Here are some common problems with subject-verb agreement:

1. Most problems with subject-verb agreement arise when a sentence contains intervening material between the subject and the verb:

   Each <u>of the men in the room</u> have filled out the application.

   The subject *each* should take a singular verb *has,* not the plural verb *have:*

   Each . . . has filled out the application.

2. Beginning writers can get confused when their sentence begins with *there* or *here*. Neither of those words can function as the subject of the verb. In such sentences the subject always comes after the verb. Consider this example with a compound, plural subject ("a lake and a creek"):

   WRONG: There is a lake and a creek in that park.
   RIGHT: There are a lake and a creek in that park.

3. Don't be fooled by false compounds, created with phrases such as *accompanied by, along with, in addition to.*

   WRONG: The manager, along with her staff, agree.
   RIGHT: The manager, along with her staff, agrees.

Compound plural subjects are created only with *and*:

   The manager and her staff agree.

4. When you have a dual subject connected by *or*, treat the subject as plural only if the noun closest to the verb is plural:

   The accountant or the bookkeepers are expected to complete that job.

   The bookkeepers or the accountant is expected to complete that job.

Pronouns also must agree with their antecedent, the word they refer back to. Here are some typical problems:

5. Intervening material causes problems:

   WRONG: Each of the boys got their applications.
   RIGHT: Each of the boys got his application. (Each . . . his. . . .)

6. The pronouns *someone, anyone, anybody, either,* and *neither* are singular.

Anybody who wants his or her [not *their*] paycheck early can collect it in the main office.

8.5 Parallel Structure

When creating lists, put the elements in the list in as similar a form as possible. The list in this sentence consists of *-ing* words:

That company prefers packaging, addressing, and loading its packages at its warehouse.

A breakdown in parallel structure looks like this:

That company prefers packaging, addressing, and to load its packages at the warehouse.

The unbalanced element in the above sentence is *to load.* The easiest solution to such a problem is to change the unbalanced element so that it matches, as closely as possible, the structure of the other elements in the list. In the example above, just change *to load* to *loading.*

Sometimes, however, the unbalanced element cannot be easily changed into the desired form:

> The company's performance last year was erratic, confusing, and with lots of ups and downs.

In this circumstance, you remove the awkward element from the list:

> The company's performance was erratic and confusing. The stock went up and down.

When editing for balanced structure, look for elements connected by *and* and *or.* In resumes, check for breakdowns in parallelism in lists of skills, job duties, honors, and activities.

Problems for Classwork and Homework

P8.1 Homophones

The food critic's column below contains errors in homophones. On a separate sheet of paper, write down the line number where each error occurs and indicate the needed correction (for example, change *to* to *too*).

It's been a long time since I have had the pleasure of eating at one of the Hot Dog Emporium chain eateries, but I stopped by the West Palm Beach site yesterday too try out their new French Dog Deluxe. Their were many people lining up for this treat, so I expected something marvelous. Unfortunately, the dog I got was to oily for me too even finish. Its skin looked and felt rubbery, to. I felt the affect of the grease for hours afterward.

Don't they know that the first principal of hot dog making is to cut the grease?

I don't know if the dogs their at the West Palm outlet are the same as everywhere else, but if so, the company's got a real dog of a product on their hands. I wasn't to impressed by the Big Dog's supposedly French sauce, either: some sort of mustard-yellow goo spread in to much quantity along the dog's top and sides, soaking into its tasteless bun. Their trying to call the bun a "French roll," but the affect of the sauce undermined that pretension.

In the hot dog business theirs not to much competition stemming from product variation, so I don't see the need for this new product. The Emporium folks should stick too they're standard fare instead of trying to get us to except exotic versions of there successful menu items. Next time I head over they're to the Emporium, I'm going too ask the personnel for a simple dog without to much mustard—theirs nothing better on a hot afternoon, is their?

P8.2 Related Words

On a separate sheet of paper, write down the line numbers where errors occur in the following text. Show how you would fix each error.

Dear Dr. Winston:

I am writing to ask for a recommendation. Although I took less courses from you than I wanted to, I was able to take you for Management II, Business Math, and Business Statistics. Between those courses, I excelled best in Management, obtaining a high A grade. I didn't lay down on the job in the math courses either, obtaining *B's* in both of them.

If you recall the report I wrote in Management II on preventing employee theft, then you know that my oral skills are excellent. I remember that you were upset that semester about the number of disinterested students in that class, many of whom didn't even bother to turn in a report. By contrast, I was extremely interested and learned a large amount of important facts and principles in that course.

P8.3 Possessives, Contractions, and Hyphenated Plurals

On a separate sheet of paper, write down the line numbers where you find a failure to use hyphens to form possessives, contractions, or hyphenated plurals. Show how you would fix each problem.

TO: Jim Sloan
FROM: Bob Stewart
SUBJECT: Keeping the managers spirits up

By the end of the month we will have enough sales to keep the managers spirits up. Childrens pets are selling fast this summer. Our sales of rats, turtles, and lizards are already greater than in all last years. Were sold out of snakes.

The two downtown stores sales have also increased, though the suburban shops sales are higher than any others. Youre going to like Peggys year end report; this years profits will top our closest competitors by 20 percent at least. So dont worry. There will be a lot of *0*s in your bonus check this year.

P8.4 Run-Together Sentences

On a separate sheet of paper, write down the line numbers in which run-together sentences occur. Show how you would fix each problem.

Cindy, I want to congratulate you on your successful bid for the bank construction project, it was a marvelous example of careful research tied to forceful proposal writing. I expect you to get a decent raise out of this, however, I can't provide details about that yet, therefore don't spread that news around. I want to get you started on another project, however, not to worry, it will not be as difficult as the one you just finished, you need a break, I can tell. Because Martin wants someone competent to work on a proposal for a playground in Louderville, I'm going to recommend you for that one.

P8.5 Agreement

On a separate sheet of paper, write down the line numbers in which subject-verb or pronoun-antecedent agreement problems occur. Show how you would fix each problem.

Dear Customer:

The order that you sent to us for seven Brazen Gold counter tops cannot be filled because it is out of stock. Neither the gold nor the red are a best seller, so we may not be getting any more in. However, every one of the other colors that you find in our catalogue are in stock or can be ordered.

Sometimes a customer who wanted gold can manage with yellow. They find that the yellow works just as well with his or her decor. A counter top with two colors blended together in patterns are nice also. A blend of two colors, both of which should match the wood work and general decor, give the top a classy look. The counter top, in addition to the wood cabinets below, are the center point of the kitchen design, and our consultants will be glad to advise you on any issue that arises.

P8.6 Parallel Structure

On a separate sheet of paper, write down the line numbers in which unbalanced structures begin. After each line number, show how you would edit out the problem.

Thank you for your interest in our products and in bringing the defects in our Newline Electric Razor to our attention. We value the opinions of our customers. Your critique of the Newline series has been passed on to the highest levels in our company and will be read and considered with great interest. Your comments were explicit, full of detail, and were cogent.

In fact, your critique was so good that we would like to hire you as a general consultant and to review our new product lines. If you are interested, send us a resume, three recommendations, and include your salary requirements. You can send us the resume immediately via e-mail or send by regular mail along with the other materials.

9

Eliminating Biased Language and Policy

For both ethical and legal reasons, you should avoid unnecessary references to race, ethnicity, religion, age, or gender in business communications. Almost all such references are unnecessary.

You should also avoid making policies or other decisions based on assumptions about the characteristics of groups. Instead, assume that differences among people arise from the uniqueness of individuals.

9.1 Avoiding Gender-Biased Phrasing

The need to keep texts free of gender-biased phrasing leads to some tricky writing problems. Not too long ago, it was the universal habit of writers of English to use masculine pronouns to refer to groups of mixed gender:

> When criticism comes from above, a good manager will take the blame for *his* subordinate.

But nowadays a sentence like the one above is inappropriate because it suggests that managers are always male. Because English lacks a gender-neutral singular pronoun to refer to people, numerous solutions have been devised to address this problem. Here are five:

1. Use *he or she, him or her, his or her:*

> When criticism comes from above, a good manager will take the blame for *his or her* subordinate.

Avoid this approach when it leads to awkward sequences of paired pronouns:

> When criticism comes from above, a good manager will take the blame for his or her subordinate, even if he or she acted without his or her authority.

2. Pluralize the antecedent and use the neutral plural pronouns *they, them, their:*

> When criticism comes from above, good *managers* will take the blame for *their* subordinates.

3. In a long text, alternate between the feminine and masculine pronouns.

> When criticism comes from above, a good manager will take the blame for *her* subordinate, even if the subordinated acted without *her* authority. In this way she will earn the subordinate's trust and *he* will be inclined to work hard for her.

Avoid this approach within a passage in which the pronouns refer to the same person:

> When criticism comes from above, a good manager will take the blame for *her* subordinate, even if the subordinate acted without *her* authority. If *he* does not do this, his subordinates will not trust *him* and may not produce for *him*.

4. Avoid pronouns by using articles and by repeating nouns:

> When criticism comes from above, a good manager will take the blame for *a* subordinate, even if the *subordinate* acted without authority.

5. Some well-educated people use plural personal pronouns *(they, their, them)* in conjunction with singular nouns and especially singular indefinite pronouns that have a plural meaning, such as *someone, everybody, anyone, anybody:*

> After training, *everybody* is to return to *their* department where *they* will train others.

This use of what is sometimes called "singular they" is considered grammatical and acceptable by some language authorities, such as the Merriam Webster editors *(Webster's Dictionary of English Usage)* and some rhetoric scholars (for example, Zuber & Reed, 1993).

However, this option is considered an error in pronoun agreement by those who take a conservative perspective on language decisions. Every large organization has its share of language "purists" who would object to singular *they* as too informal for business communications. Many writing instructors, including possibly your business writing teacher, take a conservative stance against controversial language usages. In the end, you should make your own language decisions. But you should also understand the ramifications of your choices. If you use singular *they*, for example, some readers might assume that you have made a mistake in grammar.

Before you can authoritatively assert your independence by deviating from the most widely accepted norm, you must know that norm. The assignments in this chapter, therefore, ask you to edit out singular *they, them, their* and use other options listed here for avoiding gender-biased language.

Other problems in sexist language arise from past assumptions about gender roles. Thus when the assumption is that doctors are usually male and that nurses are usually female, we hear such terms as "lady doctor" and "male nurse." Such assumptions are no longer tenable, and such language is now considered biased.

Problems also arise from the old Germanic root *-man*, meaning "human being," a root found not only in the word *man* but also *woman*. Most people, when they hear this root in words such as *chairman, policeman, fireman,* and *mailman*, feel the root conveys a masculine implication. The root *-man* seems to suggest a favoritism even in words that obviously refer to both sexes, such as *mankind*. With a little thought you can come up with inoffensive alternatives:

chairman	chairperson, chair
policeman	police officer
fireman	firefighter
mankind	humankind

9.2 Biased Policy

Discrimination against individuals or groups in the workplace is often illegal. Title VII of the Civil Rights Act of 1964 prohibits organizations that employ at least fifteen people from discriminating on the basis of race or color, ethnic identity, religion, or gender.

Amendments to Title VII have since added protection to older citizens. The Age Discrimination in Employment Act of 1967 and the Older Workers Benefit Protection Act of 1990 prohibit discrimination in hiring, promotion, and firing on the basis of age. In addition, women are further protected by the Equal Pay Act, which requires equal pay for equal work, and the Pregnancy Discrimination Act, which prohibits discrimination against pregnant women in hiring and firing and protects them from forced pregnancy leave or loss of health benefits.

Finally, the Americans with Disabilities Act of 1992 protects from discrimination those individuals defined as having "a physical or mental impairment that substantially limits one or more major life activities." It is legal in hiring to ask if a person can perform a specific job, but it is not legal to ask anyone about the existence of a disability; or if the disability is obvious, its extent.

For both ethical and legal reasons, your business communications should reflect an equal treatment of people. In some situations, however, the federal government will permit limited discrimination if it can be shown that a particular kind of person cannot do a particular job. For example, a job advertisement for models from a company that makes only female clothes could legitimately call for female applicants only, excluding males from applying.

Problems for Classwork and Homework

P9.1 Qualified Minorities

The last line of job notices often states that "qualified minorities and women are encouraged to apply." Such statements represent efforts to help certain groups who have been and often still are discriminated against. However, some representatives of these groups say that the term "minorities" is inaccurate, because there are more people of color than white people in the world and more females than males. Furthermore, even talking about minorities relegates certain people to an "outsider" status. Many women don't feel oppressed, and some of them resent being thus typified. Are these objections silly? Should the phrasing be revised or thrown out? Assume that this issue has been raised in your small company. Write a memo to your boss, Mary Saffran, presenting your view on this issue.

P9.2 Store Policies Revision

As the new manager of a large discount clothing store, you have noticed that many of the employees are young people just out of high school, with little experience in the professional workplace. In some cases, their behavior reflects that inexperience and their general immaturity. So you ask one of your older assistant managers to write up a set of employee policies—a guideline for appearance and behavior—for distribution. He produces the following document, which reflects certain biases and stereotyping and an unacceptably antagonistic tone. The document appears poorly organized as well.

Edit the document to rid it of unfair policy and biased language, and give the text a more civil tone. Salvage those policies that speak to legitimate concerns; get rid of those that don't. As you revise, reorganize so that appropriate issues are addressed under the subheadings.

PERSONNEL POLICIES FOR WEST END CLOTHING OUTLET

Employees of this company are expected to meet certain standards for appearance, behavior, attitude, demeanor, and work habits. Failure to meet those standards will lead to dismissal and no recommendation. The Asians among our employees make good models. Other employees should study their work habits and polite behavior.

Appearance

Employees are expected to show up to work in neat, semi-formal clothing, reflecting the standards of the workplace in the Civilized World. No torn jeans. No collarless shirts. Women should wear skirts and blouses. Men should wear slacks and a white shirt or formal shirt with a conservative necktie (not a big wide thing with flowers).

All females should wear enough make up to appear formal, like someone at work rather than someone who just woke up from a nap at home. No super-long fingernails. No dreadlocks.

Men should have clean hands and nails. Wear your hair cut above the ear, and no scraggly beards. No oversized Afros and no shaving your head either.

Girls can wear unobtrusive jewelry, as long as it isn't mutilation stuff like nose rings. Men are not to wear jewelry, except a ring on their finger. Keep your shoes shined.

Those who smoke—when you come back from your break or from lunch, everyone, including the customers, can smell the smoke on your skin and clothing. For this reason, smoking is no longer permitted on the premises.

Work Habits and Attitude

Employees are expected to show up to work on time. That means 9:30 a.m. or earlier for the first shift, not 9:35. Two latenesses and you're docked half a day's pay. Three and you're fired.

You get two ten-minute breaks, not three. Lunch is lunch, not a siesta.

Women should smile at the customer; men should appear earnest and competent.

Don't tell the customer that something is no good. Suggest to him that another item would suit him better. Don't ever "bad mouth" the store, even on your own time in your own home.

Sexual Harassment

No dating fellow employees. That just causes trouble. We don't want employees bringing their lovers' spats into the workplace.

P9.3 Scandal

What are the consequences of biased attitudes, policies, behavior, and language in the workplace? In November 1996, a tape recording became public in which executives at Texaco were heard talking disparagingly of

African-American employees. People got fired. The company paid 176 million dollars in compensation expenses. Find an article describing another significant scandal of this type and write a summary. Be prepared to make a brief oral report in class.

P9.4 Age Harassment

It has come to your attention that three of your employees have been talking disparagingly of older workers in the company, ridiculing their appearance, habits, and abilities, and suggesting that they should be fired to make room for younger people. Write those three a memo clarifying your company's stance against age discrimination and your own views on how colleagues should treat one another.

P9.5 Harassment Policy

Write a sexual harassment policy for a small company. Begin with a "no tolerance" policy statement followed by an extended definition that classifies different types of harassment and provides a scenario for each. Include procedures for responding to harassment at the time of the incident, filing formal complaints, protecting accused personnel, determining the facts, and punishments.

You might begin by examining the official sexual harassment policy for your school. For additional background research policies from other local organizations and read the cover article, "Abuse of Power," in the May 13, 1996, issue of *BusinessWeek*. You might also examine sexual harassment policies of U.S. companies published on the World Wide Web. Use a search engine like Altavista (www.altavista.digital.com) to search for key words such as *sexual harassment policy*.

You may use such research information to get general ideas about content, but if you borrow unique ideas you must give credit to the source, and if you copy a source's exact wording you must use quotation marks and give credit. In such cases, your instructor may require you to use formal in-text documentation and provide a bibliography. If you need a refresher course on documenting sources, look ahead to chapter 16.

10

Communicating across Cultures

The end of the twentieth century has seen a worldwide shift toward democratic governance and open markets, leading to a "global economy." Doing business with foreign companies and foreign entrepreneurs is becoming routine. The Internet has made it possible for even the smallest garage-shop business to sell its products world wide. However, communicating across cultures carries its own set of writing problems. Ignorance about cultural differences can lead to miscommunication and loss of business opportunity.

10.1 The Translation Problem

In a famous Cold War speech emphasizing U. S. support for beleaguered West Berlin, President Kennedy told an enthralled German crowd: "Ich bin ein Berliner!" Translation: "I am a jelly donut!"

The word *Berliner* can also mean "a resident of Berlin," but only if the article *ein* is dropped: "Ich bin Berliner."

Presidents have better translators than most businesses, certainly better than the small Taiwanese company, a maker of plastic parts for computers and houseware, that handed out literature at a West Coast trade fair containing the following sentences:

> [X Corporation] established in 1980 and decided to do plastic goods due to plastic have had being instead of a lot of parts and accessories of hardware and woodenware since 1980's. Which inevitable reasons are composed of light weight, thinner, shorter, smaller and mass production, especially in inexpensive pricing.

The company itself may have been better organized and more exacting in the production of its plastic products, but its production of sales literature didn't inspire confidence.

Norm Leaper (1994), in an article on translation gaffes by ABC employees, reveals the best solution to the translation problem. If you need to translate writing into a foreign language, have a native speaker of the language do or at least review the translation. Don't trust someone's book learning.

10.2 Using International Business English

Because English is the language most often used for international business, most of your communications with foreign associates will be in English. To create effective communications, you must take into account the difficulties that nonnative speakers encounter, particularly with English. Here is some general advice for avoiding miscommunication when writing in English to an international audience:

1. Avoid complicated sentences whose meaning may escape someone whose grammatical knowledge is limited to basic sentence patterns. The following sentence, with its truncated opening phrase and reduced right-branching structure, might give your reader trouble: "That project done, we can then focus on bringing in your contacts, the important link between the two enterprises." Full clauses—structures with subjects and verbs—are easier to understand: "When we have finished that project" (instead of "That project done") and "Your contacts are the important link" (instead of ". . . your contacts, the important link").

2. Avoid idioms, expressions that do not mean what the words literally say. For example, "That enterprise bought the farm" might leave a foreign colleague wondering about a real estate purchase. Avoid sarcasm, which can also lead to confusion or affront. Interpreting attempts at irony requires a sensitivity to tone that your audience may lack when struggling with a foreign language. If you say disparagingly, "Our first efforts were *wonderfully successful,* weren't they?" (meaning "quite unsuccessful"), your reader might take you literally and misunderstand. Slang words may not appear in your reader's translation dictionary. In particular, edit out verb-particle idioms, expressions that combine verbs and prepositions in idiomatic ways: "If you *run across* any additional problems with the contract that *bear on* your obligations, *run* them *by* me, and I'll *go over* them with you before you *sign off.*"

Encounter is easier to understand than *run across; related* is easier than *bear on; show* is easier than *run by; review* is easier than *go over; agree to the contract by signing* is easier than *sign off.* Nothing is wrong with putting prepositional phrases after verbs. *Run up a hill* is easy to understand. But *Run up a lot of debts* consists of a difficult verb idiom (*run up*) followed by a noun phrase.

3. Proofread carefully for spelling and grammatical errors. Native speakers of a language are able to recognize and ignore such mistakes, but nonnative speakers, operating from reference books that describe only correct forms, may be lost when they encounter an error. Avoid or explain abbreviations and acronyms. Don't use nontraditional spellings *(thru, lite)*.

4. Use standard American letter, memo, and report formats. However, be aware of cultural differences in rhetoric. *Rhetoric* refers to the development of content within texts, the ways in which meaning is constructed and conveyed. Different cultures use different rhetorics. For example, Americans like to move quickly to the point and then provide supporting detail. Asian cultures use a rhetoric that proceeds slowly to the point. For best results, modify your rhetoric to make it less foreign to your reader. For the Japanese, Korean, or Chinese reader, you might begin with pleasantries and then proceed inductively, presenting supporting information that leads up to the main point.

10.3 Cultural Difference

Experts in international communications have described in broad terms cultural differences important to communication. On the most general level, the United States, Israel, and the countries of northern Europe, especially Nordic countries and Germany, use similar rhetorics and ways of doing business. But countries in southern Europe, the Middle East, Asia, and Latin America differ in varying ways from the first group in regard to vital issues such as directness in communication and the importance of ritual.

Many other groupings and contrasts between countries and cultures are possible. Marshall Singer (inspired by Johan Galtung) divides states according to the degree to which they dominate—or have, in the recent past, dominated—their region (1987, p. 216–17). By this categorizing, the United States and Japan fall into the same classification and share a similar self-confidence.

It is important not to put too much trust in such groupings. Categories and generalizations may provide a starting point, a guide to what to look for in your research, but before you communicate with someone in Country X, you should research the specific culture of that country.

People who grow up and work in different cultures do develop different attitudes and behaviors in regard to such matters as **time** (the importance of punctuality; slow and cautious versus quick and daring approaches to business ventures); the basis for **deals** (friendship versus contracts); **decision making** (individual versus consensus decisions; shared versus unshared authority); concern about **formalities** (the relative importance of ritual and saving face); and **directness** of communication (direct versus indirect approaches to main points). You can explore these differences through library research and the Internet.

In creating a profile of a particular culture, however, it is important to go beyond academic research and seek out first-hand advice from people in your organization (or outside it) who have either grown up in, or worked in, the target country. A former citizen of the target country can provide important clues by telling you what he or she found unusual about America when first arriving. A native U. S. citizen who has worked in the country usually has valuable tips on travel and doing business there.

10.4 Cultural Chauvinism

If you are a United States citizen at this time in history, when the United States is the strongest military and economic force in the world, you may believe that people from *other* cultures should find out how *you* communicate, and that it is up to them to imitate the North-American style. And you may indeed get away with that arrogant approach. But there are at least two reasons why you are better off studying and respecting the culture of a person you deal with.

In the first place, knowledge of the culture will help you avoid misunderstandings that can undermine your own business interests. The model letters in this chapter illustrate this point (Boxes 10.1–10.4).

In the second place, your international venture is more likely to succeed if the relationship is based on genuine friendship, rather than mere necessity. In some countries, business people make deals only with people they know, like, respect, and trust on a personal level. You can begin to establish a good personal relationship with your foreign partners by learning how to communicate and behave in a manner that they will perceive as respectful.

10.5 Cross-Cultural Communication at Home

Despite the common perception of the United States as a melting pot, and despite the existence of what might be called a "shared culture" and a "common set of business practices" in the United States, many U. S. locales are dominated by racial or ethnic groups that retain their unique identity and habits, including their ways of communicating and doing business. For instance, Southern California has become the center of a rising middle-class Hispanic-American culture. The *Washington Post* quotes a successful entrepreneur from this milieu:

> A lot of corporate people . . . don't understand that our values are different. We're skeptical of government and large banks. We want personal and familial relationships. Our

Box 10.1

Model Problem: Writing to a Japanese Distributor

Your company, American Rice & Grain, Inc., has entered into a partnership with a Japanese company, Marui Trading Company, Ltd., for the purpose of exporting American grains to Japan and Korea. A year has passed and everything is going well. As the newly appointed manager in charge of this exportation, you feel the necessity to prove your worth within your organization by expanding your company's exports. Therefore, you develop a proposal to open a new market in Taiwan through your Japanese partner, and you send this proposal to your counterpart at Marui, Mr. Yoshida. (See Box 10.2, Incompetent Letter to Yoshida). In your proposal, you put forward strong arguments in support of your project, and you feel optimistic that Yoshida will be convinced and will want to join you in this venture.

Unfortunately, Mr. Yoshida's written response (Box 10.3), at first reading, is confusing at best, unenthusiastic at worst. What is Yoshida really saying? You begin to realize that you should have taken the trouble to investigate Japanese cultural differences and business practices before sending your ideas to Yoshida.

After researching Japanese cultural differences, write the proposal letter you should have written, one that would have resulted in a better start to this project. A solution to this problem appears in Box 10.4.

The "Hi" is too informal and might be seen as disrespectful.

Yoshida would likely worry about the sudden turnover, especially given the casual way in which it is being treated. He might wonder if *you* will disappear the moment an opportunity to make more money comes along.

Yoshida would not agree that jumping into a new operation would be appropriate before you have even familiarized yourself with the old.

Moving fast at the outset is not the Japanese way. The slangy idioms here might be confusing: "get our foot in the door"; "beat us to the punch."

Yoshida would not work with a foreigner by himself. He does not have the authority to make decisions on his own.

All this rushing around does not inspire confidence in your judgment. Again, the idioms may be confusing: "on board"; "nose around." The blatant failure to use International Business English shows a lack of thoughtfulness that borders on discourtesy.

Box 10.2

Incompetent Letter to Mr. Yoshida

Dear Mr. Yoshida:

Hi! I'm your new counterpart at American Rice & Grain. Your old contact, Lisa Simmons, wasn't fired; she just took a job for more money at another company. No problem. In fact, I have more authority within the company than she did, so this works out for the best.

I'm just about oriented to our present set of transactions, and everything looks good to me. Therefore, I'd say it's time to move on to the next phase. I'd like to extend our trade into the Taiwan market.

As you know, Taiwan is a booming economy, getting stronger every year. It is also a country of limited physical size. As their manufacturing areas enlarge, they are left with less and less land that can be economically devoted to rice fields and other agriculture. That's where we come in! Our advantage at this side of the Pacific is that we have lots of land that can be devoted to grain cultivation, and this situation is likely to continue indefinitely.

Furthermore, Taiwan's recent democratization adds to its stability. It's really a prime market. If we don't move fast to get our foot in the door, other grain traders from the Asian region may beat us to the punch.

Let's you and me work together on this and put through a deal with a Taiwanese broker. I can put together a significant shipment at almost a moment's notice, so there's no problem there.

I look forward to getting your reaction. If you're on board, I can fly out to Kobe and we can both shoot down to Taipei together and nose around.

Box 10.3

Mr. Yoshida's Response

Dear ______:

I am delighted to hear from you, especially now when our mutual business is flourishing. We couldn't have managed such success without your earnest efforts; we appreciate doing business with you.

The letter begins with a traditional formal courtesy, the expression of joy at the success of the reader's business operations.

Thank you very much for sending us your proposal for expanding our distribution of American grains to Taiwan. This is a very interesting idea. Your reasons were quite cogent. I personally enjoyed reading your proposal and I admire your thoughts on the possibility of expanding to Taiwan.

Expressed this way, the turnover communicates greater respect for Marui, not instability with American Rice & Grain. There is a promise of permanace: "from now on."

Establishes the mutual goal of a long-term relationship.

No doubt such an expansion would be profitable. This is an idea that I am sure our management will consider in the future as a possible project.

Delicately and inductively raises the issue of expansion to Taiwan. This plants the seed of an idea without pressing for a response. The inductive approach—providing reasons to support the idea, then the idea—makes the rhetoric "friendly," less foreign.

Let us enjoy the success that charaterizes our new business partnership. We look forward to a long relationship with American Rice & Grain.

Recognizes the need to work with the whole management team, not just Yoshida, and the desire of Japanese business people to socialize before negotiating. This letter will not convince the executives at Marui to jump quickly into a new operation, but it will leave them with better feelings about you and your ideas, and in the long run that may expedite matters.

Box 10.4

Solution to Model Problem: Appropriate Letter to Mr. Yoshida

Dear Mr. Yoshida:

I am pleased to hear of the success of the Marui Trading Company in its various enterprises.

Because of the success of our mutual grain import operations, our company has decided to place a person of higher authority in charge at our end. Therefore, I will be your contact at American Rice & Grain from now on.

I am pleased that our operations have been so successful, and I look forward to a long, mutually profitable relationship with the Marui Trading Company.

As I contemplate the situation in Asia, in general, I am impressed by the recent advancements in Taiwan. It is now a politically stable democracy with a growing economy. It is our feeling at American Rice & Grain that such countries are potentially good markets.

As our grain distribution business continues to flourish, we may eventually want to expand operations. Perhaps some time in the future we can talk about Taiwan as a possible next step in our Asian distribution efforts.

I look forward to meeting you and your colleagues next month when I am in Kobe so that we can begin to get to know each other on a personal level.

> first call is an introduction call. We do business with handshakes. We don't sue each other. We tend to back away from paperwork. (Cannon, 1997, p. 33)

When published sources on these regional groups are not available, you can sometimes get a start-up profile by studying their homeland cultures. For example, Glen Fisher (1992), in his book *Mindsets,* provides a description of the business mentality found throughout Latin America that closely matches the *Post* article's information on the California subculture. But again, it makes sense to consult with a member of the cultural group, or with someone who has experience working with the group, instead of relying on "book knowledge" alone.

10.6 Communicating with the Japanese: An Extended Example

In chapter 13 on responding to complaints, you will be advised not to apologize if you are not at fault. That's because in the United States an apology usually means, "I did something wrong that hurt you, I regret that you have been hurt, I admit that I am to blame, and I will try not to do it again."

The Japanese, by contrast, apologize more frequently, but to them an apology often means, "I genuinely regret that my actions have caused you distress. However, I am not entirely at fault, my actions were not the sole cause of your trouble, and I probably won't change my behavior." To the Japanese speaker or writer, the act of apologizing signals regret over a breakdown of harmonious relations. The apology is an attempt to regain harmony.

Obviously, communication mishaps can occur when commonplace gestures like apologizing have such different meanings.

Edward and Mildred Hall (1987) discuss Japanese culture as it pertains to verbal behavior in detail in their book *The Hidden Differences: Doing Business with the Japanese,* a good example of literature that can help you communicate across cultures. But be careful. The Halls, for instance, are not Japanese, and their research depended on their own—inevitably imperfect—interpretation of what Japanese "informants" were telling them. As with translations, try to get a native to review any cultural profile you develop as a guide for communicating cross culturally.

A comparison of Japanese and United States cultural differences yields important contrasts, among them:

1. LONG TERM VS. SHORT TERM The Japanese prefer long-term business relationships. They want to develop trusting relations as opposed to

purely contractual relations. They are cautious, in no hurry, and don't expect immediate results. They hope that the American in charge of a mutual venture will remain in charge, just as their own contact person will continue in that position, partly as a result of their system of life-time employment. Their employees receive no pressure for immediate results. Americans tend to want to make money fast. The turnover is much higher in U. S. companies, where sometimes only quick results are rewarded. Americans will press for a quick deal, relying on contracts in place of deep or long-term relationships.

2. INDIRECT VS. DIRECT EXPRESSION For any complex negotiation, the Japanese prefer an indirect rhetorical approach in which the writer approaches the main point slowly and perhaps never directly states it but merely suggests or hints at the intended message. The Japanese are educated in a school system that expects students to figure things out for themselves, and Japanese adults expect readers to get the point without being told everything explicitly. Direct questioning about the obvious is considered childish; direct expression of the obvious, condescending. Americans are more apt to ask dumb questions "just to make sure," and, in writing, they value clarity and try to make their points "idiot proof." Americans see opaqueness as a stylistic flaw.

3. POLITENESS VS. CONFRONTATION The Japanese abhor rudeness and explicit confrontation (and seem to Americans to be excessively polite). One reason for their indirect rhetoric is to allow uncomfortable messages to be softened by a haze of pleasantry and courtesy. The Japanese believe in saving face at all costs; they don't seek to crush and humiliate those with whom they disagree. American rhetoric, derived from the classical Greek and Roman forms of legal disputation, is much more blunt and confrontational. The purpose is to win an argument. Through debate clubs, American schools offer training in winning. Formal debating is far less common in Japanese schools and in the society as a whole.

4. WIN–WIN VS. WIN–LOSE The Japanese don't want to win arguments; they want to reach a compromise agreement. Out of their Buddhist transcendentalist tradition comes a desire to find a unified vision above the level of base conflict. They don't see conflict as a struggle between good and evil, as in the drama of Western religion, but rather as the consequence of incomplete understanding on the part of both sides.

The Japanese use a consensus form of decision making within their own organization, and then work for consensus with their outside partners. If you push your views too strongly, the Japanese will see you as rude and childish. The Japanese consider compromise as the adult approach to problem solving. They seek win–win, rather than win–lose outcomes.

Although Americans also sometimes resolve issues this way, they often use means other than consensus. Either the boss makes the decision or the individual assigned to the task is given the independent responsibility of solving problems and making decisions. In many American organizations individuals rise or fall on the basis of their individual successes or failures. As a result, some American business people are necessarily pushy and aggressive, traits that are not admired in Japanese business circles, where even overt enthusiasm may be frowned upon.

5. COLLECTIVISM VS. INDIVIDUALISM The Japanese see you as indistinguishable from your company. Your mistakes or failures are your company's, and your company's are yours. You will lose respect if you criticize others in your organization or if you try to disassociate yourself from your organization by refusing to take the blame for someone else's mistake. Americans are more likely to see themselves as independent entities working for an organization for as long as it is mutually beneficial, and no longer.

Again, these are only generalizations or tendencies. They don't take into account unique personalities, which exist even in strongly conformist societies such as Japan. And more important, as we develop closer economic ties with nations like Japan, inevitably our ways of doing business gravitate toward each other and become less distinct. American companies like General Motors' Saturn employ a management system similar to those found in Japanese manufacturing companies. And as the model Japanese complaint letter in Box 10.5 reveals, the Japanese have adopted the American rhetoric for routine business letters—straight-to-the-point organization and blunt style.

Problems for Classwork and Homework

Note: Some of the problems in this section refer you to World Wide Web sites. If you run into sites that no longer exist, follow the process described in chapter 26, section 26.4: Handling Outdated Site Addresses.

P10.1 Translation

You have written the following thank-you letter to a new contact in Germany:

> Dear Herr Schmidt:
>
> Thank you for your kind hospitality while I was in Germany. You were a perfect host and I enjoyed meeting your family, especially your charming wife, Hilda. What a great cook! You are a lucky man.
>
> I particularly enjoyed our visit to the Bavarian Alps. I hope when you come to the United States I can show you our

Box 10.5

Japanese Complaint Letter

Heisei 8 February 14

Matsui Office Supplies
Shipping Department Supervisor, Tanaka Hideo

Kobe-shi Chuo-ku Mita-cho 2-33
Fukuya Co. Ltd.

Section Chief Ikawa Giro ○

I am omitting opening courtesies.

We received the F-200 file folders that we had ordered from your catalogue after seeing a sample you had sent to us.

The products we received, however, seem different from the sample. We believe that they are inferior. There is no way for us to comfortably sell this product. Therefore, we are returning the shipment collect.

Upon your examination of the shipment and your consideration of this matter, please promptly send us the correct products, which match the sample.

In haste.

Enclosure: one invoice.

The end.

In Charge: Products Control Section, Mikami.

The letter is addressed to Mr. Hideo Tanaka at Matsui Office Supplies

Section Chief is the rank of the writer's supervisor. The circle represents the location of Mr. Ikawa's personal signature stamp. The stamp indicates that the supervisor reviewed the letter. This convention reflects the degree of group participation in decision making and the lack of independence for managers.

The conventional term *Ijo*, translated here as "The end," signals the end of text.

Because the letter began with the conventional phrase *Zenryaku*, form requires that it end with another conventional phrase, *Soso*, translated here as "In haste," meaning that a hasty conclusion corresponds to a hasty beginning.

The year is expressed as the 8th year since the latest emperor has been in power (Heisei is the name that will be given to him after death)

Return address: City of Kobe, Chuo ward, the Mita block of 2nd St, no. 33. The name of the company (Fukuya) comes last.

The body of the letter begins with a conventional phrase (*Zenryaku*) indicating that all traditional opening courtesies will be omitted. Otherwise the letter would have to make a flattering comment about the reader's company.

Mikami is the writer's last name. His first name doesn't appear anywhere in the letter.

gorgeous Rocky Mountains. The German beer halls were wonderful. I think we got more business done there than in your office building!

Thank you again, and I hope to see you soon in the United States.

A person in your office was a German major in college, so you ask her to translate your letter into German, because Schmidt speaks only a little English and his wife speaks none at all. Your colleague produces this version:

Lieber Herr Schmidt:

Ich danken Sie für Deine schöne Gastfreundlichkeit weil ich war in Deutschland. Du warst ein perfekter Gastgeber und ich habe genossen, Deine Familie zu treffen besonders Dein charmantes Weib. Was für eine großartige Köchin. Du bist ein glucklicher Mann!

Insbesonders habe ich unser Besuch zu den bayerischen Alpen genossen. Ich hoffe, wenn Du zu den USA kommst, ich kann dir unsere imposanten "Rocky" Berge zeigen. Die deutschen Bierhallen waren wunderbar. Ich denke, we haben mehr Geschäft dort erledigt dann in Deinem Heschäftsge-baude.

Danke schön noch einman und ich hoffe, Dich in den USA bald zu sehen.

Find a native speaker of German (perhaps a professor or an international student) and have the translation checked. Report to the class on any embarrassing errors in the translation.

P10.2 International English

An assistant of yours wrote the following business letter, destined for Chile, and passed it on to you for approval. Revise it into International Business English. Replace obscure vocabulary with ordinary language, change the idioms into literal statements, and simplify the syntax where appropriate. As part of creating a rhetoric less foreign to your reader, make the letter more dignified by remove phrasing that is too informal.

Dear Mr. Gomez:

Greetings from the old U. S. Upon arriving back at my office, I found your report in the mail, a welcome sight, one that reminded me immediately of the pleasant times I had in Santiago. When you come to New York I hope we can chow down and toss a few at my favorite Irish watering hole.

The report looks good. I see that you were able to talk the Endago Co. out of the outlandish requirements they had attached to the purchase of their undeveloped acreage. There wasn't a snowball's chance that my company would go along with their having nonrescindable right-of-way access, in perpetuity, throughout property we intended to develop.

I welcome working with you on this project. I think that both our companies are going to make out like bandits. Or should I say, "banditos"! See you in March.

P10.3 Egypt

Your boss, Francis Williams, is leaving for Egypt next month to discuss a joint venture with prospective Egyptian partners. Williams is busy boning up on details of the business deal he hopes to pull off, and he has asked you to research Egyptian culture and report in a memo what he should know about this subject before traveling abroad.

a. Research and write that memo. A good starting point would be the "Business Travel" section for Egypt within the Arab Web site at www.arab.com. Your teacher may require you to use one or more additional sources.
b. Assume that your boss became ill and you must go to Egypt. On the basis of your research, compose a letter to your Egyptian counterpart, Mohammad Akbar, introducing yourself and discussing your expectations for your meeting with him. Use International Business English and an approach to business and business writing that will make Mr. Akbar feel comfortable.

P10.4 Woman Alone

You work for the international charitable organization Medicine for Mothers, and your boss, Yoshiko Miller, is planning a tour of several countries in Central and South America in order to enlist corporate sponsors for national branches. Vaguely aware of the *macho* attitude of the stereotypical Latin male, Miller is concerned about how businessmen in these countries will treat a female professional. She also worries about socializing as an unaccompanied woman. Finally, born in Japan (she's the widow of an American), she wonders how the Central and South Americans will react to her Asian identity. She has asked you to research these subjects and write her an informative memo report. A good starting point would be the epilogue in Lawrence Tuller's *Doing Business in Latin America and the Caribbean* (New York: American Management Association, 1993). Your teacher may require you to use one or more additional sources.

11

Making a Personal Request

Routine requests, such as asking a company to send you a price list, are straightforward and cause writers little trouble. But personal requests can get tricky. A personal request is one in which you ask someone to do something special for you. Such requests often amount to asking for special treatment, such as additional services or exemption from a policy. Even a simple request for a favor—"Johnson is sick; can you stand in for him at the meeting this afternoon?"—can get complicated if, for example, Johnson was supposed to report at that meeting.

The requests you will deal with in the homework section of this chapter have the kinds of built-in complications that so often arise in everyday transactions. Be sure to pay attention to all of the significant contextual details of each request.

11.1 General Advice

When making a personal request, follow the "three-part principle" for organizing short communications: a beginning that orients the reader, a middle that provides details, and a closing section that makes it easy for your reader to fulfill your request.

Personal request communications should maintain a tone that is respectful—not groveling, pleading, complaining, demanding, or threatening. A respectful tone in this kind of communication can be achieved through a slight formality, punctuated with a compliment or two, provided the compliments don't sound forced. If you can do anything to make it easier for the reader to fulfill your request, work that into the middle or last section.

11.2 Possibilities for the Beginning

People may feel irritated if they sense that you're being coy about stating what you want from them. Therefore, after your opening sentence or phrases, which might orient the reader to your identity and to the situation, you should move fairly quickly toward making your request in general terms. Add to this section some flattering statements, if appropriate, but avoid sounding obsequious.

11.3 Possibilities for the Middle

The middle section spells out your request in specific terms and how the reader can perform the service requested. Most of the details go here.

11.4 Possibilities for the End

The final section might present additional arguments in favor of granting your request. This is your last chance to persuade. The last section might also include important details about how the request can be fulfilled, such as where something should be sent. The communication might also close with a specific request for further contact and discussion. An optimistic conclusion is usually appropriate for this kind of communication.

11.5 The You- and We-Perspectives

In order for your request to succeed, your reader must have an interest in agreeing to it. Try to imagine why your reader should want to help you. What does your reader have to gain? Focus as much of your text as you can, gracefully, on your reader's interests. This is called taking the "you-perspective." The model letter in Chapter 2, Box 2.3, provides an example. The writer is asking a shop owner to carry a particular product. He ends the letter promising to become a regular customer if his request can be fulfilled.

Taking the *you* perspective can also mean focusing your message generally on the reader. The *I* perspective, conversely, focuses on yourself:

I Perspective:

> I saw a room papered in the Professional Perl wallpaper, and I think that this color and style would be best for our offices. I like the quiet tone and conservative look that it provides. It makes me feel relaxed, yet ready to concentrate on work.

You Perspective:

> The Professional Perl wallpaper represents the quiet, conservative, professional style that you prefer. Its atmosphere will make you feel relaxed, yet ready to concentrate on work.

In addition to the *you* perspective, you can cultivate a *we* perspective, in which you join the reader's interests with your own: what's in it for *us*. If asking a supplier to consider changing a shipping policy, for example, you might begin by saying: "It is in our mutual interest to speed up delivery of orders. . . ." Or, if asking a professor to give you a short time extension on an assignment, you might talk about the two of you being partners working toward the same educational goals. You both want the educational process to result in a successful project.

Problems for Classwork and Homework

P11.1 *You* Perspective

Analyze the model solution in Box 11.2 in terms of the "*you* perspective." Do this simply by counting the number of "me" pronouns, singular and plural (I, me, my, we, us, our), and comparing that total with the number of "you" pronouns (you, your). Not every use of a "you" pronoun will constitute a gesture to the interests of the reader, but some will, and the overall count will give you a sense of whether or not the writer is paying attention to the reader or merely talking about himself.

P11.2 Real Request

Find an actual personal request letter or memo. Your instructor may have left one or more on reserve in your school library. In a memo to your instructor, describe how closely the sample document follows the three-part structure recommended in this chapter.

P11.3 Foreign Food

As the foreign student adviser, you are concerned with the daily living problems of the fifty international students on your campus. At this time, the majority are Chinese, with some Japanese and Thai, and a few Latin Americans. These students, especially the Asians, have been complaining to you about their inability to find ingredients for their kind of cooking in Big Value, the one small supermarket in your college town. They can get these ingredients in a nearby city, but almost none of them have cars and riding the bus requires an all-day expedition. They wonder why the local store doesn't carry even basic items such as sesame oil, rice wine vinegar, bok choy, fresh ginger root, and wonton skins.

Box 11.1

Model Problem: Personal Request

Your camp, along with six other vacation homes, is located on a flat mountain top called Long Point in Southwestern Pennsylvania. The eighty-acre wooded area lies off a state road and is served by a single, narrow, gravel road that dead ends. During the winter, the county sends up a huge truck with a plow after each substantial snowfall. The driver plows one side of the gravel road on the way in and the other side on the way out, leaving driveways blocked by a huge ridge of plowed snow. These are vacation homes; most residents get up there for a weekend of cross-country skiing or hunting only occasionally during the winter, and it is common for them, upon arrival, to find ridges across their drives piled five feet high with several layers of plowed snow that have frozen solid.

After meeting this past summer with your Long Point neighbors to discuss this problem, you have volunteered to contact the person who drives the truck to request that, each time he plows the road next winter, he pause to break an opening in each of the driveways. You have been authorized by the other residents to offer him a reasonable "tip" in return for this extra service. Compose a letter making this request, addressed to Everett Nickles. Invent addresses for Nickles and yourself.

The first sentence identifies the writer and brings up the context of the request. The writer then compliments the reader, so that the point about the trouble being caused won't sound like criticism. Note the neutral "snow plowing," instead of an accusatory "your plowing." The request comes at the end of the first section.

In the middle section the writer seeks the reader's empathy by presenting details to clarify the nature of the problem.

Then the writer attempts to win the good will of the reader by empathizing with him. Finally, in this middle section, the writer proposes a solution to the problem, returning to the request and offering recompense for fulfilling the request.

The last section establishes a procedure for fulfillment of the request. By giving the reader a local phone number, the writer avoids asking the reader to undertake the expense of a long-distance call.

Box 11.2

Solution to Model Problem

Dear Mr. Nickles:

The six other residents of Long Point and I are pleased with the snow clearance you provide each winter. After each storm you are there promptly making our camps accessible. However, snow plowing also creates a problem for those of us who only occasionally get up to Long Point. The ridges that the plow makes across our driveways accumulate and freeze. Would it be possible for you to pause in your plowing and break an opening in the ridges across the seven driveways each time you plow our street?

Permanent residents are able to easily shovel or even plow their cars through the small ridge your truck leaves behind after each plowing. But we part-time residents aren't there to handle the problem while it is manageable. By the time one of us gets to his or her camp, you may have plowed the road several times, building the ridge of snow blocking the driveway to four or five feet, each layer freezing so that the snow cannot be tossed aside with a snow shovel.

We realize that in fulfilling your contract with the county you have a large territory to cover and many roads to clear, and that most of the work has to be done early in the morning so that the roads are ready for morning traffic. Perhaps you could do our road last when you aren't under any time pressure. We're willing to pay you for your inconvenience and extra effort—say $5.00 per resident each time you plow. That would come to $35.00.

If this solution is amenable to you, Mr. Nickles, could you leave a message on my answering machine at Long Point. The number there is 722-5555. If you cannot find the time to perform this extra service, perhaps you could recommend someone.

Thank you for considering our request.

You have had a nodding acquaintance with the manager of Big Value, Percy Dobbs, for many years, and he knows your name and that you work at the college. You are quite familiar with the stock at this store: it is consistently bland, a "white-bread" line of products that seems to appeal to the townsfolk. Write Mr. Dobbs a letter asking him to consider adding a line of Asian food products. Invent addresses.

P11.4 Request for Credit

Your landscaping company is gearing up for a new big contract you just landed. You will be planting wild flowers, bushes, and trees in the divider for a 210-mile section of the interstate highway in your state. Unfortunately, you don't have the cash to purchase all the soil products and vegetation that you'll need. Write a letter to your main supplier, Mason Greenery, asking for supplies on credit. This company has a policy of payment up front. The owner is Mac Polanski. Invent addresses and letterhead stationery.

P11.5 Whitworth Recommendation

As a junior at Mon River College, in a small town outside of Pittsburgh, you wish to ask a particular instructor, Dr. Emma Whitworth, for a recommendation for a unique summer internship. You will work as business manager for a pilot version of a summer-work program sponsored by the federal government. College students entering the program that you will manage can pay off student loans by doing public service work. As business manager for this pilot program, you would be rubbing shoulders with presidential aides. Who knows, you might even get invited to the White House.

Unfortunately, you happen to know that Whitworth is working on a research study of family leave policies in Pittsburgh-area corporations and is extremely busy. In fact, although she is frequently on campus to use the mainframe computer and her office, she is officially on leave this semester to finish up her study. Nevertheless, you believe that Whitworth respects your work, and you feel certain that you must get her recommendation in order to land the job. You have excellent qualifications, but so do other local applicants. Whitworth is a respected scholar and her support will give you a good chance. Application materials for this position are due May 5, two months from now (date your letter March 7). Write her a "letter of request" asking her to write you a recommendation. Invent addresses.

12

Complaints

You have undoubtedly purchased a product only to find that it doesn't work, or breaks easily, or doesn't do what it is supposed to do. And you have probably experienced bad service of some kind or other. You may have shrugged off such incidents as a part of living in the modern world, but companies cannot always afford to do so. When your business or organization receives inadequate products or services, you may be obliged to seek restitution to avoid a loss of money.

12.1 Appropriate Tone

Complaints usually call for a slightly formal tone, to make sure that the reader knows that you are serious. Be polite and optimistic, even if you are feeling frustrated and angry. Until you find out otherwise, assume that this unfortunate situation is unusual. Typically, people who sell products or provide services regret inconveniencing their customers and want to correct any problems.

Your courtesy will be appreciated, making it more likely that you will reach a satisfying solution. See Boxes 12.1 and 12.2 for an example of a strong but polite complaint.

12.2 Possibilities for the Beginning

Begin your letter by identifying yourself as a customer and by naming the service or product (including model number or specific type). Establish the general nature of your complaint, including the time frame (when you became a customer; when the problem occurred).

12.3 Possibilities for the Middle

Continue your letter with specific details about what happened. In the case of a defective product, convince the reader that the breakdown cannot be attributed to your lack of knowledge, or incompetence, or misuse of the product. You might mention the inconvenience you suffered, but don't dwell on it. Focus on clearly describing the problem. Indicate which aspects of the product or service were satisfactory and which aspects were unsatisfactory.

12.4 Possibilities for the End

Conclude your letter with a clear statement of what you want the reader to do to satisfy you or how you and the reader can work together to solve the problem. If possible, finish with an upbeat, optimistic closing statement.

Problems for Classwork and Homework

P12.1 Campus Problem

Identify a problem around campus (for example, bad food in the cafeteria, inadequate parking, poor registration procedures, lack of course offerings in your major). Write a letter to the proper authority making a complaint and suggesting one or more solutions.

P12.2 Highway Breakdown

You recently took your one-year-old car to the Boca Raton dealer you had bought it from and asked him to do a grease and oil job and look over the engine because you were taking a long trip. Now, a few days later, you are driving 65 miles per hour on the Florida Turnpike when you smell something burning. You notice that your heat gauge is stuck at the hottest level, and you look up to see white smoke breezing back from your hood. You pull off on the next exit just as a loud clack-clack sound emerges from the engine. Your only good luck is that you spot a service station at this exit. The personnel there hose down your engine and, once it has cooled enough, they look it over. They discover that the water hose has broken. When you mention that you asked your dealer to have the engine inspected while doing a grease and oil job, the service station mechanic comments that the car has not been greased.

Your bill for replacing the water hose, putting in new oil, and doing a grease job comes to $44.50. At the motel that night you decide to write a letter of complaint to your car dealer back home: Herb Paulson, 566 Spanish Creek Road, Boca Raton, FL 33431. Write that letter. Invent a home address for yourself in Boca Raton.

P12.3 Canine Castle

Because you once had a bad experience with a pet dog dying of a congenital disease, you always purchase your dogs from respectable breeders who make sure that their dogs' lineages are free of such diseases. That's why a year ago you paid Canine Castle $450 for Apple Butter Boy, your Chocolate Labrador Retriever, $100 above the normal market price. Unfortunately, Apple Butter Boy has developed hip dysplasia, a genetic disease common to Labradors. It is crippling unless corrected by a five-hundred-dollar operation. His other hip could collapse at any time as well. Your warranty on the dog guarantees your choice of either recompense in the amount paid for the dog or a new puppy. The assumption in these warranties is that you will be putting your damaged pet to sleep. However, Apple Butter Boy is now a member of your family, so you can't have him killed. The cost of saving Apple Butter Boy is going to exceed the $450 you originally paid for him. Furthermore, you are upset about the fact that Canine Castle, knowingly or unknowingly, is using defective dogs in its Labrador breeding line, despite their advertising claims to the contrary. Write a letter of complaint to the folks at Canine Castle. Invent addresses.

P12.4 Italian Wine

Your wine distributorship, Fate of the Grape, Inc., sells cases of high-quality imported wines to stores across the United States. Lately you have been having trouble with your Italian supplier, Fratelli Roppolo (Via Ubricci #15, Latisana (Udine) 33053, Italy). Cases of Merlot have been arriving late, some not at all. As a result, you have been unable to fill some orders, and you worry about losing customers.

You have always relied on the Roppolo brothers, who are both sommeliers, to pick good wines for you. But, although the rest of the reds and all of the whites they've been sending you have been fine, the Merlots have been bland to nearly tasteless. Judging by the labels, the brothers have lately been buying their Merlots from small local vineyards rather than large, well-known wine producers. That could be a factor, or perhaps all Italian Merlots are declining in quality at this time.

Write a letter of complaint to the Fratelli Roppolo company. Try to communicate your concerns clearly, without offending. These agents have provided you with good service in the past, and you don't want to have to go to Italy and search for a replacement. On the other hand, you are displeased, and you want the problem solved. One of the brothers, Ernesto, speaks fairly good English, but you should use International Business English (see chapter 10, section 10.2).

Box 12.1

Model Problem: Complaint

Assume the role of Rudi Hauser, the owner of Rudi's Country Store. You hired the lowest bidder, American Paint Company, to paint the outside of your store. You ended up having a lot of problems with the paint crew (invent details), and there was an overcharge — you were billed for a can of paint the workers had spilled on your parking lot. Write a letter to the owner of American Paint Company complaining about their service and asking for an adjustment in your bill.

Identification of the service and the problem

Details about what happened

What the writer wants

Optimistic close

Box 12.2

Solution to Model Problem

Rudi's Country Store
R.D. 1
Ft. Mark, PA 15540
August 22, 19__

Mr. Franklin Morrison
American Paint Company
537 Schoolyard Road
Messina, PA 15540

Dear Mr. Morrison:

I am writing to you because I have been unable to reach you by phone, even after leaving messages on your machine. Your painting crew just finished painting my store and I am not entirely satisfied with the job or the bill.

Your workers tended to arrive late, about 9:30 a.m., and leave early, about 3:30 p.m. Once they missed a whole afternoon because, according to the foreman, they had another job to do. As a result, they were on site for four days instead of the estimated three.

The crew's behavior on the job was also unnecessarily disruptive. They worked with no shirts on and yelled to each other. My store stays open until 10:00 at night, and I would have appreciated it if they had cleared away their empty paint cans and other paraphernalia from around the front and sides of the store after work every day, but instead they left each afternoon without cleaning up.

I also seem to have been billed for a can of paint that the workers overturned, staining the parking lot. I fixed the stain, but I would like my bill adjusted accordingly. I hope you will pass these complaints on to your foreman. Because you are a successful company, I am sure that these practices are not normal. Your bid was low, and the paint job looks good. I look forward to doing business with you again, if you can assure me that the problems I mentioned will not arise.

Respectfully,

13

Responding to Complaints

Any complaints that your organization receives from customers should be answered quickly and politely. If you need time to look into a situation, say so in your initial response, but don't delay that response. The model letters in this chapter provide examples of both positive and negative answers to complaints.

In addition, your organization should have formal procedures in place to allow subordinates to make serious complaints such as harassment or discrimination charges. For the sake of the employee and the company, those procedures must be followed.

13.1 Taking Advantage of Complaints

Complaints may be unwelcome, but you can turn them around to your own advantage. Customers, for example, are often pleasantly surprised and impressed by a quick correction of a problem, and such action can promote good will for your organization. Complaints also give you an opportunity to communicate with customers while you have their close attention. Look for subtle ways to promote your company. Finally, complaints can serve as a starting point in identifying and correcting your organization's internal problems.

13.2 Apologies

Before you respond to a complaint, analyze the situation to determine if you or your organization is at fault, and if so, what the proper corrective response should be. A quick, knee-jerk apology is rarely the best action. Never apologize if you are not at fault. In contrast to the Japanese style of communication (see chapter 10), in our culture an apology means that you accept blame and responsibility. If you are, in fact, at fault, and no basis exists for being sued, apologize.

13.3 Tone for Complaint Response

The proper tone for complaint responses is one of earnest regret, even if the problem isn't your fault. Whatever the situation, you can sympathize with a customer who is having trouble. When you admit fault, do not grovel—maintain dignity.

13.4 Possibilities for the Beginning

When you begin a letter in response to a complaint, apologize, if you are wrong; otherwise, commiserate. Indicate what you will do, or what the reader might do, to rectify the situation. If possible, put in a good word for your organization.

13.5 Possibilities for the Middle

If the complaint is about a service, you may wish to explain what happened from your perspective, without making excuses. If the complaint is legitimate, indicate what your organization is doing to handle the problem and to ensure that such problems won't arise in the future. If possible, put in a good word for your organization (see Boxes 13.1 and 13.2).

If you must reject a claim for an adjustment, such as a requested refund for a "faulty" product or a reduction in a charge, specify exactly why you cannot make the adjustment. You may have to delicately point out that the customer misused the product or failed to carefully read advertising literature when selecting the product (see Boxes 13.3 and 13.4 for an example). Requests for adjustment generally come from customers, people whose good will you want to keep. Bear that in mind when phrasing a rejection.

13.6 Possibilities for the End

End your letter by stating exactly what you will do to satisfy the customer, if anything. Apologize again, if you were in the wrong. Repeat your regret that the writer is having problems. If possible, put in a good word for your organization.

Problems for Classwork and Homework

P13.1 Analyze Complaint Response

Find and analyze an actual business letter in response to a complaint. Your instructor may have left one or more on reserve in your library. Write a memo to your instructor describing the degree to which the letter follows the advice given in this chapter on structure, content, and tone.

P13.2 Respond to Your Own Complaint

If you wrote a letter of complaint in solving one of the problems at the end of the previous chapter, write a letter of response to that complaint. Assume the role of the person to whom you had addressed your complaint letter.

P13.3 Choose a Problem

Choose one of the complaint problems that you did not work on in the previous chapter. Imagine the letter that would have been written and write a response to it.

P13.4 Student Complaint

You are the department chair of the graduate program in school counseling. You just received the following letter from an older student, Martha Peters, complaining about one of your department's most competent professors:

> I would like to lodge a formal complaint against Professor Cloris Baron, whom I took this past semester for Legal Issues in Counseling. Professor Baron apparently had it in for me from the beginning. She didn't like any of the answers I gave during in-class discussions. Nor did she like any of the essays I wrote for her on the exams. And she gave me an F on my research paper, even though I spent countless hours in the library putting that paper together.
>
> I believe that what we are dealing with here is a personality conflict. My work was not graded fairly. I wish to appeal for a grade change. I think that I deserve at least a C in the course, not the F that I received.

You discussed the matter with Dr. Baron, who gave you her explanation for the grade. Martha Peters missed five out of fifteen night-class meetings. She failed the objective parts of the exams, not just the essay parts. Her research paper was sloppily written, it contained numerous examples of plagiarism on the phrasing level, and the documentation was done completely wrong. She was the only member of the class who failed to turn in a rough draft for review. If she had, many of the problems with her paper might have been avoided.

Write a negative response to the Peters complaint. Treat her like a customer making a request for an adjustment. Inform her of her right to appeal.

P13.5 Lawn Damage

As the secretary for the Volunteer Fire Fighters' Association for your county, you have been given the responsibility of responding to the following letter, which recently arrived at your Brimwood fire house. Do so, inventing addresses.

Dear Sirs:

I wish to complain about the behavior of your men last week as they put out the fire at 545 Green Street. That house is directly across from mine. One of your trucks left an enormous gouge in the front corner of my lawn when trying to maneuver into position.

Your men left behind smaller gouges in my lawn from their boots and various equipment. They also left behind a general mess of water-logged debris of various kinds.

I would appreciate it if your crew would come over here and fix my lawn to its previous condition. I also hope that you will be tearing down the charred remains of my neighbor's house fairly soon; they are a danger to local children and an eyesore to the neighborhood.

Sincerely,

Arthur Pippin

Arthur Pippin

Box 13.1

Model Problem: A Justified Complaint

You are the owner of the American Paint Company, and you just received a letter of complaint from Rudi Hauser (Box 12.2). Write a response to that complaint.

Apology and response to the customer's request

Explanation without excuses

Further indication of what will be done, in response to the customer's request

Sales pitch

Apology repeated

Box 13.2

Solution to Model Problem: Responding Favorably to a Complaint

American Paint Company
537 Schoolyard Road
Messina, PA 15540
August 25, 19__

Mr. Rudi Hauser
Rudi's Country Store
R.D. 1
Ft. Mark, PA 15540

Dear Mr. Hauser:

You are quite justified in being upset about the service you received from the American Paint Company, and I apologize for the inconvenience you endured. I have adjusted your bill, reducing the amount to account for that can of paint the workers spilled. A new invoice is enclosed.

If the paint stain in your parking lot needs further work I will be glad to send my other foreman to remove it.

I want you to know that the problems that you experienced do not represent how we normally do business. Because we have been successful at satisfying customers, our business is growing, and the crew we sent to your store was brand new; this was their first job. Because of difficulties at another site, the foreman who was supposed to be breaking in this new crew had to be at this other site to help out. I was out of town on business, which is why your phone calls weren't answered.

I have already talked to all our foremen about your case, and I can tell you that we will never again send out an untrained crew without supervision.

Mr. Hauser, I hope that you will give our company another chance the next time you require painting services. We did underbid the other companies you requested bids from, and in the future you can be sure that you will receive the best service from a company that normally prides itself on the way it treats customers.

Again, I apologize for your inconvenience.

Sincerely yours,

Box 13.3

Model Problem: An Unjustified Claim for Adjustment

Your company, Computer Universe, received this e-mail message requesting a refund:

> Dear Computer Universe:
>
> I just bought your computer screen saver, Mountain Climbers, at a price of $15.00, and I am dissatisfied with the product.
>
> The program has no timing control, and the pictures flash on the screen in sequence, one after another, much too rapidly. I don't get to enjoy the pictures. If I had known that the pictures were timed this way I never would have purchased this screen saver.
>
> I would like a full refund. Please tell me how I should proceed to return your product. I purchased it by visiting your Web site, entering my credit card number, and then downloading it.
>
> Sincerely,
>
> *Brad Gleeson*
>
> Brad Gleeson
> bgleeson@nof.com

Reject this claim for an adjustment.

Box 13.4

Solution to Model Problem: Rejecting a Claim for Adjustment

Dear Mr. Gleeson:

We regret that you are dissatisfied with the Mountain Climbers screen saver. It is one of our inexpensive savers and does not have a timing control, as you correctly point out. Only our $30 savers allow you to control the timing of the pictures. That fact is stated in the paragraph describing and contrasting the features of the $15 and $30 models.

In order to avoid customer disappointment, we allow those who visit our Web site to test the screen savers in advance of buying them. Somehow you must have overlooked that offer, which appears as one of the options on our main menu. If you had tested Mountain Climbers, you would have seen the speed at which the pictures change.

Because you downloaded the product, it is impossible to return it. Therefore we cannot give you a refund.

Again, we are sorry about your disappointment. We hope that you will continue to consider our screen savers in the future, and that you will take advantage of our "Test a saver" option on the main menu.

Sincerely,

Leon Spinner

Leon Spinner
President

Good-News Messages

This chapter focuses on messages that arise entirely out of pleasant circumstances. For example: "Our hiring committee has selected you . . ."; "I appreciate the good job your workers did . . ."; "Sally, your work record has been excellent over the past two years, and therefore I am going to recommend you for a promotion . . ."; "Your article has been accepted for publication in *Manufacturing News*. . . ." Box 14.1 provides a model.

14.1 Two Key Principles

When you pass on good news, follow two key principles:

1. Put the good news up front—don't delay it.
2. Use the message as a means of expressing and gaining good will. In some cases, it is even appropriate to include a sales pitch.

14.2 Possibilities for the Beginning

Open your letter with a greeting and then present the good news in general terms. The tone should reflect your own pleasure in conveying good news to the reader.

14.3 Possibilities for the Middle

Use the middle of your letter to provide details about the good news. Openly express your pleasure at the reader's good fortune and at being able to present good news. Seek the reader's good will. If appropriate, include a sales pitch for your company.

If you must add any bad news or necessary qualifying of the good news, include that in this section. Follow this with a review of the good news so that the text ends on a positive note.

14.4 Possibilities for the End

Reassert your pleasure and good will. Request action if appropriate (for example, "Sign the original and one copy of the contract and send it to . . .").

Problems for Classwork and Homework

P14.1 Winning Bid

Your business supply company, Total Office Outlet, has decided to rewire a large section of its building in order to handle the expansion of floor space devoted to digital and electronic products. You sent out a call for bids, and Brown Electric's bid of $9,560 was the lowest. Write a letter to Brown Electric that states the good news and indicates the necessity of setting up a meeting between you and their representative to iron out details about the timing of their work. Address the letter to the owner, Twyla Brown. Slip in a sales pitch. Use letterhead stationery and invent addresses.

P14.2 Good Gardener

After tripping on your own curb, you were laid up this summer with a sprained ankle and broken toe. This was a particular hardship for you because you enjoy caring for your elegantly landscaped yard. You hired a neighbor's teen-aged son, Tim Weiss, to care for your yard and spent considerable time explaining to him his complex duties. Still, you assumed that he wouldn't have your green thumb or your fanatical concern for detail, and you expected deterioration.

To your surprise, Tim did a marvelous job. Write a letter to his father and mother, George and Carol Weiss, expressing your gratitude and praising their boy. Invent details.

P14.3 Hiring Niece

You are the manager of River Walk, which includes an exclusive shopping center, boat docks, a small park, and other amenities along the river that runs through a large U. S. city. This is a city government job, so the local press scrutinizes hiring practices. For that reason you felt distinctly uncomfortable when your niece, Priscilla McDonald, applied for an accounting position you had advertised. Fortunately, her credentials were far superior to those of the other applicants, and she impressed not only you but the other two members of the hiring committee at her interview. You feel quite justified in hiring her. Write her a letter offering her the position. In the middle section, provide enough detail so that she knows that she got the job on merit.

P14.4 Article Acceptance

As the editor of *Making Moola,* a hip magazine for those who like to take chances and have fun by investing in or undertaking unusual enterprises, you are pleased to accept Ralph Toner's article describing his winter weekend business of drilling holes for ice fishermen on Lake Crystal. Toner scoots around on his snowmobile with his gas-powered auger on the back, drills holes, rents fish-line holding devices, and sells coffee. He makes more than $500 most Saturdays and almost that much on Sundays. His article does require some changes. For example, the text is too long. You want to eliminate the part about his wife complaining that he's never home on weekends, but you want to expand the part about his dog guarding his base on the shore while he's making trips on the ice, perhaps with an anecdote. One possibility is an incident in which his dog saved his coffee machine from a thief. Write Toner a letter of acceptance that includes the required revisions.

P14.5 Favorite Teacher

Good teachers affect many people's lives, but they don't always know when it happens. Sometimes good teachers who work hard but don't feel appreciated burn out and quit. Or they reduce their level of commitment and effort. It helps when students communicate genuine respect and appreciation.

Select a favorite teacher from school or college (but not your current business writing teacher). Assume that you have just graduated from college and landed a good job. Your future looks secure. Write this teacher a letter expressing your appreciation for his or her contribution to your growth as a person and development as a student.

P14.6 Increased Compensation

You are the president of Ocean World, a chain of three aquatic zoos, one each in Florida, Ohio, and Iowa. You have heard grumblings about a possible strike from workers who feel that they are underpaid. To head off this undesirable event, you have decided to increase salaries by a small percentage and to add certain benefits to every employee's compensation package (especially benefits that will cost little or nothing, such as free passes to the facilities). Write a memo to all employees announcing this good news. Invent details.

Box 14.1

Solution to Model Problem

Turn around the model problem in Chapter 12 and assume that the workers did an excellent job. Write a letter of appreciation to the owner of the company.

Rudi's Country Store
R.D. 1
Ft. Mark, PA 15540
August 22, 1998

Mr. Franklin Morrison
American Paint Company
537 Schoolyard Road
Messina, PA 15540

Dear Mr. Morrison:

The opening states the good news in general terms.

Your painting crew just finished painting my store and I am very impressed by the work that they did for me.

The middle presents the details.

Not only does the paint job look wonderful, but also your workers operated in a way that minimize the inconvenience to me and my customers. They arrived early, worked steadily, and left late, so that the job took only two days. They dressed and behaved like gentlemen, and cleaned up each evening after work.

While offering a kindness to the reader, the writer also arranges to have the reader send him potential customers and puts in a subtle sales pitch for his own store.

Please feel free to send your potential customers to my store to see the work that your company does and to hear a testimonial from me. And if you ever need any of our products, I'll give you our preferred customer's price.

Respectfully,

Rudi Hauser

Rudi Hauser

15

Delicate and Bad-News Messages

In the workplace you may have to communicate messages that are certain to make the receivers uncomfortable. These messages generally flow downward in the hierarchy. For example, as a manager, you may have to advise a new employee that she is dressing inappropriately for the office, or one of your team leaders that he is too dominant in conference discussions and needs to listen more and be more tolerant of differing views.

Often you will communicate these messages orally, in the privacy of your office. Sometimes, however, you will prefer to write them, if only because writing allows you to choose your words carefully as you discuss a complex situation.

15.1 Appropriate Tone

The most appropriate tone for sensitive communications is one of tact and kindness. Try to blunt the hurt as much as possible. Include praise, if possible. Workers who are upset will not perform at their peak. In the worst case, if they feel truly insulted, they may become your enemy and work against you or against the organization behind your back. You need the good services of every employee, and this desire for good relations should always guide your phrasing.

15.2 Direct versus Indirect Approaches

In any message that contains bad news of any sort, you have a choice between a direct and an indirect approach to getting across the central message. In general, the direct approach is better if the reader knows that bad news may be in the offing. For example, if you are writing to someone who has interviewed for a job, but hasn't been chosen, there is rarely justification for keeping that person in suspense. The reader expects a yes or no answer out of your letter and wants to know immediately which it is. You might begin with this kind of sentence: "Thank you for applying for a job in the accounting office of the Panama City Parks & Recreation Department, but we cannot offer you a position at this time." You would then go on, as a matter of courtesy, to explain why you cannot offer this person a job at this time and to offer encouragement in his or her job search.

The indirect approach is preferable when the receiver has no idea that bad news is coming. This method calls for the use of a buffer, an introductory section that eases the reader toward the bad news and provides a context that will make the uncomfortable message seem reasonable or even inevitable, given the circumstances.

15.3 Possibilities for a Direct Approach

Begin a direct-approach letter with the bad news, followed by a statement of regret. In the middle, explain why the bad news is necessary. If appropriate, show how the problem lies in the situation, not in the personal qualities or actions of the reader.

In the end, express regret again. If possible, help the reader solve his or her problem. If a customer wants a product you no longer sell, suggest a substitution. If a job applicant isn't appropriate for an opening, but might work out in another position, suggest that the applicant reapply for the other job. If you can't help, wish the reader good luck.

15.4 Possibilities for an Indirect Approach

The opening section of an indirect letter contains a buffer. It is important to remember that the buffer is not just a delaying action; it is a context that will make your concern about a problem or situation seem reasonable. You might praise the reader while leading up to the problem, but make sure that you don't mislead the reader into thinking that he or she is about to receive good news.

As you shift toward the middle section, you might begin with a transitional phrase that signals a change from the pleasant to the unpleasant: "However, . . ." At some point in the middle section, deliver the delicate message. While phrasing your letter with respect for the reader's feelings, don't make the mistake of being too coy. Be certain that the message comes across clearly, or you'll end up having to deliver it again, probably more bluntly after the situation worsens.

In the conclusion you might express optimism that the problem will be solved, or suggest a solution. If appropriate, praise the reader or indicate that the reader's services to the organization are appreciated. Try to end on a positive note.

Boxes 15.1 and 15.2 provide an example of an indirect approach.

Problems for Classwork and Homework

P15.1 Racquetball Odor

Pete Patterson, a competent male executive in your marketing department, likes to play racquetball during his lunch break, instead of eating lunch. He goes to the gymnasium around the corner. Unfortunately, in a rush to get back to work before the end of his lunch hour, he doesn't always have time to shower after play and sometimes simply towels off before dressing. When this happens, employees have a hard time not pinching their noses when he stands nearby or sits next to them at a conference table, especially since the office air tends to be stuffy. Write a delicate memo to him informing him of the problem and suggesting a solution. As a way of varying this memo from the model (Box 15.2), build Patterson up by finding a way to use his athleticism as a positive force within the company.

P15.2 Super Candidate

As the chair of a hiring committee in your department, you were impressed by Rebecca Hernstein's credentials and by her interview. However, she and all the other good candidates lost out when a super candidate with dream credentials applied for the job and wowed everyone at her interview. Write a letter to Ms. Hernstein turning her down for the job. Invent details.

P15.3 Friend's Daughter

You are the managing director of your town's public library. Each summer you run a summer literacy program for disadvantaged children that involves them in extensive reading and writing. The kids create their own magazine. They research and write the articles themselves and lay out the magazine on a computer. Each summer you hire a local college student, typically an English or journalism major, to run the program.

This year, your best friend's nineteen-year-old daughter, Samantha Newkirk, has applied for the summer job. You sense in her cover letter an enthusiasm for working for you and a feeling of confidence about getting the job. Unfortunately, Samantha's cover letter and resume are sloppily done, and she doesn't have an adequate academic background, or necessary experience, or any discernible knack for the kind of work she would be doing.

Write a letter to Samantha, whom you know well enough to address by her first name, rejecting her for the position. Don't treat this as a routine rejection of a job application. Use an indirect approach and create a context for the bad news.

P15.4 Nepotism

You are the chief executive of ABC Management, a company that takes over troubled schools and runs them for profit. Against your better judgment, you let one of your managers, Julip Dauman, persuade you to hire her mother, Martha Dauman, to work as an assistant to one of Julip's own secretaries, Midori Green. This puts Green in the awkward position of having to boss around the mother of her own boss.

And indeed, ever since Martha Dauman started work as an assistant to Midori Green, Martha has driven Midori crazy. (You invent the details.) You told Julip Dauman that you would hire her mother only temporarily to see how it worked out and warned her of the inherent difficulties of this unusual case of nepotism. As a courtesy, before you fire Martha, write Julip Dauman a memo saying that it hasn't worked out and that her mother will have to go. Use an indirect approach, creating a context for the bad news.

P15.5 Rumor Control

Relations have deteriorated between management and members of the janitorial staff in your company due to protracted and acrimonious contract negotiations. As the company ombudsman, you are in the middle. One problem has been a flurry of rumors, completely false, that has spread confusion, fear, and anger among the workers. (Invent the rumors as a class, group, or individual activity.) Write a memo to all janitorial workers that debunks these rumors. Ask employees to consult with you about any new rumors before spreading them. To be effective in this situation, you need to be firm without appearing to speak for management.

Box 15.1

Model Problem: Delicate Message

Lulu Larson, a competent executive in your marketing department, wears expensive clothes, heavy makeup, and strong perfume. That is her style. The perfume, unfortunately, is too strong for many office workers. Sensitive individuals have a hard time not pinching their noses when she is standing nearby or sitting next to them at a conference table, especially since the office air tends to be stuffy. Write a delicate memo to her asking her to tone down the perfume.

The buffer begins with legitimate praise.

The buffer then creates a broad nonpersonal context: stuffiness of the offices and the difficulty arising from many types of odors. The request that she moderate her perfume should now seem logical, within that context.

Upbeat ending

Box 15.2

Solution to Model Problem

Memo

TO: Lulu Larson

FROM: Rick Stover

DATE: March 16, 20__

SUBJECT: Dealing with our stuffy environment

Thank you for setting a good example with your dress and grooming. Your professionalism is appreciated. A new man in the office can take a tip on such matters from many of the other men he sees around him, but when another woman joins our organization, she will have only you to look to for guidance. As the only woman executive, you must be a leader and must set the standard.

As your supervisor, I want to help you in any way I can. And on one matter, I need your help.

Right now I am concerned about the fact that our offices are particularly stuffy. Since we work side by side, we have to be careful about odors that may cause others discomfort, such as cigarette smoke, cologne, or perfume.

The heavy perfume you prefer fits well with your formal, dressy style, but in our cramped and airless quarters, it may cause a problem for others. In these circumstances, moderation becomes a necessity.

I know I can trust your judgment about this. You have proven yourself to be a quick learner and an effective member of our team. I am sure that as more women are hired into executive positions, you will make an excellent mentor.

16

Background to Reports: Documenting Sources

When you draw unique information, ideas, or phrasing from another person's work, you should indicate to your reader the source of your borrowing. This is called documenting sources.

Borrowings from in-house texts (from within your organization) constitute an exception. They are not usually documented, because all writings done at work are considered the property of the organization. Writers often take large sections from other in-house documents and insert them into their own documents, without any indication that such insertion is taking place. However, the writing you do in your business writing course will include material borrowed from outside sources, and that borrowing should be documented.

Professional organizations in various academic disciplines have developed their own conventions for documentation. Popular style choices for business writing are:

- American Psychological Association (APA) style; see the *Publication Manual of the American Psychological Association*
- *The Academy of Management Review* (AMR) style, published annually in its January issue and on the Web at http://www.aom.pace.edu/amr/style.htm
- Chicago style; see the University of Chicago Press's *Chicago Manual of Style*
- Modern Language Association (MLA) style, found in the *MLA Handbook for Writers of Research Papers.*

If you do on-the-job writing that requires documentation of sources, you will have to learn and use the system preferred by your organization, if it has settled on a standard. For each school course, ask your instructor which method you should use.

For reasons of space, this chapter looks at only two approaches, APA style and MLA style. APA serves many social sciences and is popular among business departments. MLA style is familiar to many students; it is often used in high school English classes and college composition courses. When you understand how one system works, you can easily shift to another. Looking at two styles side-by-side will help you see how, despite minor variations, all methods of documentation provide essentially the same information and provide ways to deal with the same problems and complexities.

16.1 The Two-Part Character of Documentation

Writers document sources in two places: in the text, close to any mention of the borrowed material; and, unless the document includes footnotes, at the end in a bibliography, a list of sources. In APA style, the bibliography is called References; in MLA style, the bibliography is called Works Cited (neither uses the generic term Bibliography).

The in-text documentation appears as parenthetical notes:

APA: Some computer companies go out of business because they are too successful and cannot meet orders (Martin, 1992).

MLA: Some computer companies go out of business because they are too successful and cannot meet orders (Martin).

The APA style gives the author's name and the date of the publication; the MLA approach leaves out the date. All the information you need to get a copy of Martin's text is listed under "Martin" in the References or Works Cited section at the end of the document.

Every in-text citation should match exactly with a bibliographical entry, and every bibliographical entry should match exactly with an in-text citation. Do not put entries in your bibliography that you read but did not refer to in your text. Your bibliography is a list of works cited, not a list of works read.

16.2 The Basics of In-Text Parenthetical Citations

This chapter shows the APA and MLA approaches to the most common citation forms and problems. A complete explanation of all issues regarding in-text parenthetical citations can be found in the *Publication Manual of the American Psychological Association,* 4th edition or the *MLA Handbook for Writers of Research Papers,* 4th edition. Both texts are available in your campus bookstore and library, and probably also at your school's writing center.

In parenthetical references, you provide the minimum information necessary for the reader to find the proper source in the bibliography. In both APA and MLA style you always provide the author's name, if that name doesn't appear nearby in the text. In both styles, when you are quoting or paraphrasing, you must provide the page number(s).

16.2a Commas in Parenthetical Notes

APA generally uses commas to separate parts of entries:

> They are important factors, but none of them is "relevant to pricing" (Smith, 1998, p. 56).

MLA generally does not:

> They are important factors, but none of them is "relevant to pricing" (Smith 56).

16.2b Citing More than One Work by the Same Author

In APA style, if you cite more than one work by a single author, the date provided might distinguish such publications. If the author is cited for more than one publication appearing in the same year, you distinguish between them by attaching a lowercase letter to the date in the parenthetical reference to match the same letter in the date in the References at the end of the document. For example:

APA: They are important factors, but none of them is "relevant to pricing" (Smith, 1998, p. 56).

In MLA style, that problem is solved differently. You include the first word or two of the title in each parenthetical note so that the reader can pick out the intended work in the Works Cited list:

MLA: They are important factors, but none of them is "relevant to pricing" (Smith, "The Pricing" 56).

Notice in this unusual case that the MLA citation uses a comma.

16.2c Bringing in the Author's Name

It is generally better to introduce the author's name in the text rather than in the parenthetical note.

APA: Smith (1995b) points out that some computer companies go out of business because they are too successful and cannot meet orders.

MLA: Smith ("The Pricing") points out that some computer companies go out of business because they are too successful and cannot meet orders.

16.2d Page Numbers

Include page numbers when you are quoting or paraphrasing. APA style uses "p." or "pp." in front of page numbers and requires the entire set of numbers when the quotation goes more than one page (pp. 587–589). MLA uses no "p." or "pp." and shortens page numbers (587–89).

APA: Jones (1996) believes that "start-up computer companies should get professional management as soon as possible" (p. 567). He also argues for borrowing enough to make the gamble reasonable (p. 572), so that, for example, the company "can get parts in large quantities cheaply from overseas suppliers" (pp. 587–589).

MLA: Jones believes that "start-up computer companies should get professional management as soon as possible" (567). He also argues for borrowing enough to make the gamble reasonable (572), so that, for example, the company "can get parts in large quantities cheaply from overseas suppliers" (587–89).

Note the order of elements with quotations: the parenthetical note is placed between the end quote and the period:

APA: . . . suppliers" (pp. 587–589).

MLA: . . . suppliers" (587–89).

16.2e Long Quotations/Multiple Authors

Long quotations (four lines or more) are indented and set without quotation marks. The parenthetical citation appears outside the end period in both styles. In APA style, illustrated below, citations with five or fewer authors list all authors' names in the first reference to their work. This is recommended for MLA, as well.

APA:

> With the salaries reaching to 120 million for a five-year contract, basketball appears to be the most lucrative sport, for men, that is. And Hamilton, Greising, Walker, and Melcher (1989) point out the difficulties in creating a women's league:
>
> > The trick is to build on the sport's growing—but still mostly regional—fan base. That's something past efforts couldn't accomplish. In the late 1970s the Women's Professional Basketball League drew poorly. (p. 52)

After the first reference, use the last name of the first author followed by "et al.":

APA and MLA: Hamilton et al. believe that . . .

For both styles, use "et al." for even the first reference to more than five authors. For two authors always cite both names; never use "et al."

16.2f No Author

When the source has no author, both styles call for the use of the first few words of the bibliographic entry, which is usually the title:

APA: Furthermore, "There's plenty of room for mistakes, delays, and cost overruns in the supply chain that stretches from raw materials to delivered product, as anyone involved in corporate logistics can attest" ("Supply-Chain Secrets," 1995, p. 77).

MLA: . . . logistics can attest" ("Supply-Chain Secrets" 77).

16.2g Quoting Quotations

Sometimes you may wish to repeat a statement that someone else has quoted. Suppose, for example, an author named Headley quoted another author named Danson. Headley wrote:

> According to Danson, "People become millionaires by working 14-hour days" (p. 81).

Suppose, now, that you didn't have access to the text Danson wrote and you wanted to use his quote in your text. APA and MLA have slightly different ways of handling this:

APA: Danson says that "People become millionaires by working 14-hour days" (as cited in Headley, 1989, p. 12).

MLA: Danson says that "People become millionaires by working 14-hour days" (qtd. in Headley 12).

Notice that the page number, 12, is the page in Headley, not Danson, because the Danson text is not available and will not appear in your bibliography. The Headley text will appear in your bibliography.

16.2h Citing Multiple Sources

Often writers, in an appeal to authorities, cite more than one source to back up a point. In both APA and MLA, use semicolons to separate the authors' names:

APA: Economies of scale have made garage-shop computer companies a relic of the past (Brim, 1995; Winston, Hughes, & Marks, 1992; Smith, 1995a; Smith, 1995b).

MLA: Economies of scale have made garage-shop computer companies a relic of the past (Brim; Winston, Hughes, and Marks; Smith, "The Demise"; Smith, "Small Companies").

Notice in APA the use of the ampersand (&) when listing multiple authors of a work.

16.3 The Basics of Bibliographical Entries

Start the bibliography on a new page at the end of your document. Center the title, References or Works Cited. List the entries in alphabetical order by the author's last name. Alphabetize works with no author by their title, ignoring *The* and *A(n)*.

APA Reference entries are formatted like regular paragraphs in manuscripts to be submitted for publication, but you can use "hanging paragraph" form for in-house reports and other writings that will not be submitted for publication. Published works using APA style always present bibliographic entries in hanging paragraph form, and that is how they are formatted in the models in this book. Always use hanging paragraphs for MLA style. With hanging paragraphs, the first line starts in the left column and every other line is indented, as in the model bibliographies on page 119.

16.4 Documenting Internet Sources

This section presents the basics for APA and MLA styles of Internet documentation. Consult your teacher or librarian on how to cite the specific index and full-text computer services your school library has purchased. Additional information and models can be acquired in the *Publication Manual of the American Psychological Association,* Fourth Edition, and the *MLA Handbook for Writers of Research Papers,* Fourth Edition. You can also find information on Internet documentation at these Web pages:

APA: http://www.apa.org/journals/webref.html
MLA: http://www.mla.org/main_stl.htm

16.4a In-Text Citations

For in-text citations, use the same format and provide the same information that you would for print sources. The idea, remember, is to connect the reader to the corresponding entry in the alphabetized list of citations in your bibliography.

The American Psychological Association, at its Web site, recommends handling personal e-mail communications as personal communications, for which no bibliographical entry is included in the list of references. By contrast, the MLA does want a corresponding works-cited entry. Here is how personal e-mail communications should be handled in-text:

APA: Ed Norwood (personal communication, June 14, 1998) described in detail the packaging process used at his branch of U.S. Steel.

MLA: Ed Norwood described in detail the packaging process used at his branch of U.S. Steel (E-mail to the author).

16.4b Templates for Bibliographical Entries

The following templates can be used to handle any situation that arises. Most teachers, well aware of the difficulties that students face in documenting Internet sources, are willing to help if you have trouble.

APA Template

The APA asks that you begin Reference citations by presenting the same information you would for a print source, insofar as that is possible, and then add the computer information. After the print-citation information, first identify the type of publication in brackets. Then write the

Model Bibliographies
with emphasized punctuation

APA Style		MLA Style
References		Works Cited
Andrew, J. M., & Prichert, J. S. (1978). Business highways. New York: Mason.	Book with two authors.	Andrew, Jason M., & Joan S. Prichert. Business Highways. New York: Mason, 1978.
Cathert, W. (1995). Defining sexual harassment. In P. Smith & D. Sauer (Eds.), Contemporary issues for our times. (pp.78–89). Miami: South Florida University Press.	Article in a book. Eds. means editors. UP means University Press. 78–89 are the page numbers where the article appears in the book.	Cathert, Wilson. "Defining Sexual Harassment." Contemporary Issues for Our Times. Eds. Paul Smith and Dick Sauer. Miami: South Florida UP, 1995. 78–89.
Fitzer, L. (1987). Investing wisely in the '90s. Business Trends 12 (3), 67–80.	Article in a journal paginated by issue. Vol 12, issue 3.	Fitzer, Lawrence. "Investing Wisely in the '90s." Business Trends 12.3 (1987): 67–80.
Holland, M. (1990). Sell less, make more. Sales Quarterly 8, 456–472.	Article in a journal with continuous pagination throughout the volume.	Holland, Misty. "Sell Less, Make More." Sales Quarterly 8 (1990): 456–72.
Kurtz, M. (1994, March 22). My first million. Today's World News 14, 45–53.	Article in a magazine. APA requires the vol. number (14 in the example).	Kurtz, Minnie. "My First Million." Today's World News 22 Mar. 1994: 45–53.
Lanham Steel stock fall. (1993, October 12). Daily Record [New Orleans], pp. B1, B3.	Newspaper article, no author. Non-continuous pagination.	"Lanham Steel Stock Fall." Daily Record [New Orleans] 12 Oct. 1993: B1+.
Lupus, M. (1990, January 14). Business cycles and the Fed [Editorial]. St. Petersburg Express, p. A8.	Newspaper editorial, late edition.	Lupus, Mark. "Business Cycles and the Fed." Editorial. St. Petersburg Express 14 Jan. 1990, late ed.: A8.
Lupus, M. (1996, January 14). What's good for business. Investment World, 32, 12–13.	Another article by Mark Lupus. The name is repeated in APA, but not in MLA.	---. "What's Good for Business." Investment World 14 Jan. 1996: 12–13.

date of retrieval followed by the type of computer source and its address or access information:

> . . . [Newspaper, selected stories on line] Retrieved January 2 1997 from the World Wide Web: http://www.sntimes.com/a1

MLA Template

The MLA provides this fourteen-point template at its Web site (reprinted here with permission of the Modern Language Association):

1. Name of the author, editor, compiler, or translator of the source (if available and relevant), reversed for alphabetizing and followed by an abbreviation, such as *ed.,* if appropriate
2. Title of a poem, short story, article, or similar short work within a scholarly project, database, or periodical (in quotation marks); or title of a posting to a discussion list or forum (taken from the subject line and put in quotation marks), followed by the description *Online posting*
3. Title of a book (underlined)
4. Name of the editor, compiler, or translator of the text (if relevant and if not cited earlier), preceded by the appropriate abbreviation, such as *Ed.*
5. Publication information for any print version of the source
6. Title of the scholarly project, database, periodical, or professional or personal site (underlined); or, for a professional or personal site with no title, a description such as *Home page*
7. Name of the editor of the scholarly project or database (if available)
8. Version number of the source (if not part of the title) or, for a journal, the volume number, issue number, or other identifying number
9. Date of electronic publication, of the latest update, or of posting
10. For a posting to a discussion list or forum, the name of the list or forum
11. The number range or total number of pages, paragraphs, or other sections, if they are numbered
12. Name of any institution or organization sponsoring or associated with the Web site
13. Date when the researcher accessed the source
14. Electronic address, or URL, of the source (in angle brackets)

16.4c Specific Bibliographical Entries

The example below shows how the templates in 16.4b can be used to form a specific bibliographical entry for an Internet source. The example is for a document taken from a personal Web site:

APA: Ohmann, S. (1996, April 20). New traps still hurt animals. Retrieved November 14, 1997 from the World Wide Web: http://www.members.nez.politico/rights.htm

MLA: Ohmann, Sterling. "New Traps Still Hurt Animals." Home page. 20 Apr. 1996. 14 Nov. 1997 <http://www.members.nez.politico/rights.htm>.

Additional examples can be found at the APA and MLA Web site addresses named at the beginning of section 16.4.

16.5 Avoiding Plagiarism

One reason for documenting sources is to avoid plagiarism. Plagiarism is the theft of intellectual property by presenting another's unique ideas or data or phrasing without acknowledgment, as if those ideas or data or phrases were your own.

It is not always easy to know whether you need to document ideas. If an idea appears in a number of texts—if it is part of the general conversation within a discipline, even if limited to experts—you can present that idea without documenting the source you found it in. If you are unsure of whether an idea you are reading is widely discussed, play it safe and document the source. Sometimes you may want to document the source of an idea that is in the public domain simply to show that your views are supported by one or more outside experts. If you cannot paraphrase entirely in your own words, writing from memory and understanding of the original text, then you should use quotation marks liberally, to avoid plagiarism on the phrasal level.

Problems for Classwork and Homework

P16.1 Article Summary

Read a short article in a business journal or magazine. Summarize the article in one or two paragraphs, quoting phrases occasionally, as in the example in section 16.2d. Demonstrate your understanding of parenthetical referencing by correctly adding citations to the paragraph (APA or MLA style, whichever your instructor prefers). Write a bibliographical entry below the paragraph for the work summarized. Because you have only one entry, use the singular term *Reference* or *Work Cited* for the title of the bibliography.

P16.2 Long Quotation

Do P16.1, but put in a long quotation, as in the example in section 16.2e.

P16.3 Write a Short Bibliography

Find a business book, an article in a business magazine or journal, an article in the business section of a newspaper, and an Internet source and write up a bibliography for these sources. Use APA or MLA, as your instructor prefers.

P16.4 Working Bibliography

Choose one of the topics below (or your instructor may assign one) and write a short "working" bibliography (five to eight entries) for a report on the selected topic. A working bibliography is a list of works that you intend to examine as you research a subject. Use APA or MLA, as your instructor prefers.

a. The future of the "information superhighway"
b. The mid-'90s decline in Asian economies
c. What business executives believe about American high school education
d. Defenders and opponents of the MSAT
e. The glass ceiling
d. The effect of anti-affirmative-action rulings on minority contractors
e. Is NAFTA working?
f. How might a space station be good for American business?
g. A topic of your choice

17

Visuals

The term *visual* refers to a pictographic approach to conveying information. Visuals provide a dramatic and clear way of revealing the meaning of information. This chapter looks at visuals that don't require professional art or layout skills, such as those commonly found in business reports. Nowadays, most visuals can be generated by computer word processing, database, or graphics programs.

17.1 Graphs

Graphs show changes and comparisons using X and Y axes. The X-axis is the horizontal line, the Y-axis is the vertical line. In a simple graph, the X-axis is marked by textual (nonnumerical) identifiers, such as company names or increments of time, as in Figures 17.1 and 17.2. The Y-axis shows

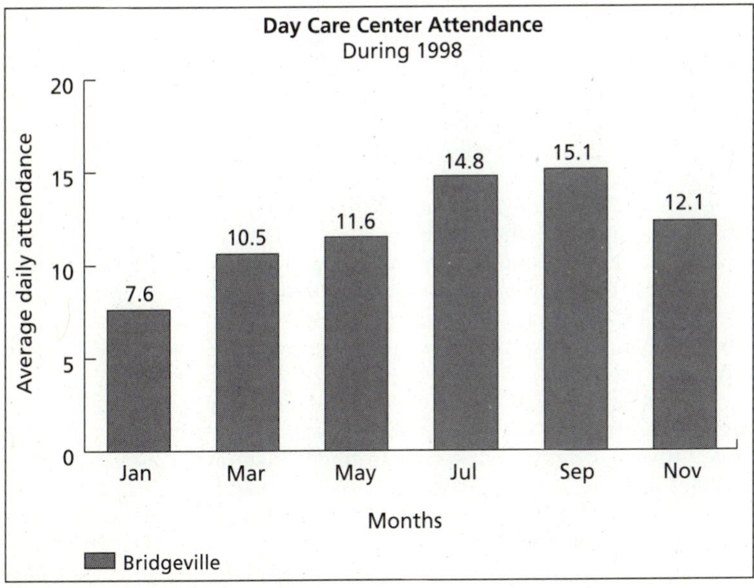

Figure 17.1 Simple Bar Graph

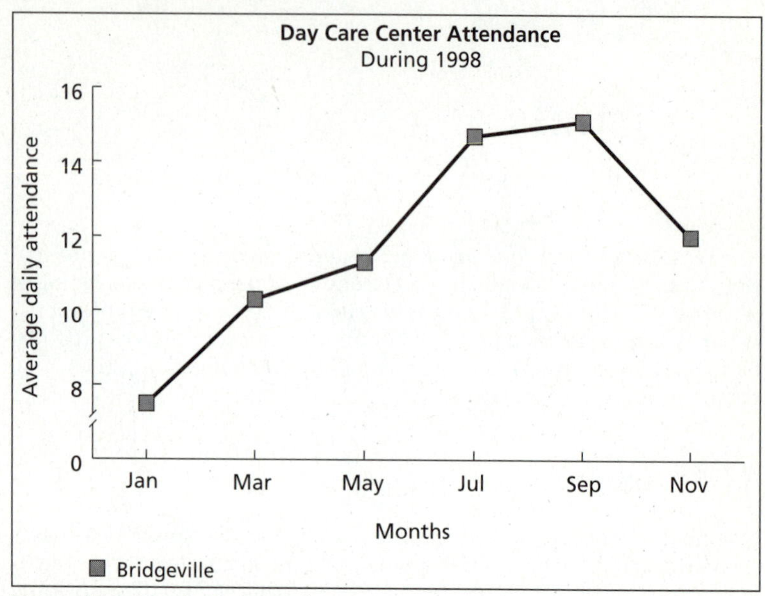

Figure 17.2 Simple Line Graph

numerical changes. For visual effect, writers sometimes rotate graphs (turn them on their side) so that the textual entries lie along the Y-axis and the numerical entries along the X-axis. Thus, a bar graph may have bars shooting out horizontally from the Y-axis instead of rising from the X-axis.

A graph might compare the performance of one entity over time (Figures 17.1 and 17.2), or it can make multiple comparisons, as in Figure 17.3, which compares the performance of two entities over time.

In a correlational graph, both the X-axis and the Y-axis display numerical changes. This kind of graph compares items by showing correlations. Figure 17.4 shows that as you add months to the length of your auto financing loan, you pay a higher interest rate. As one figure goes up, the other goes up.

Sometimes the Y-axis begins with an initial jump larger than the other increments. For example, if graphing growth in student population of a large university, most of the change might take place in a range from 18,000 to 22,000. If you used increments of 500 and started from 0, your line graph would be overly tall (you'd have to have 36 increments before getting to 18,000). Therefore, you would be wise to skip to 18,000 as your first increment, as in Figure 17.5. When you do that, you alert your reader to the jump by putting a jag or break in the Y-axis (note the base of the Y-axis in Figure 17.5).

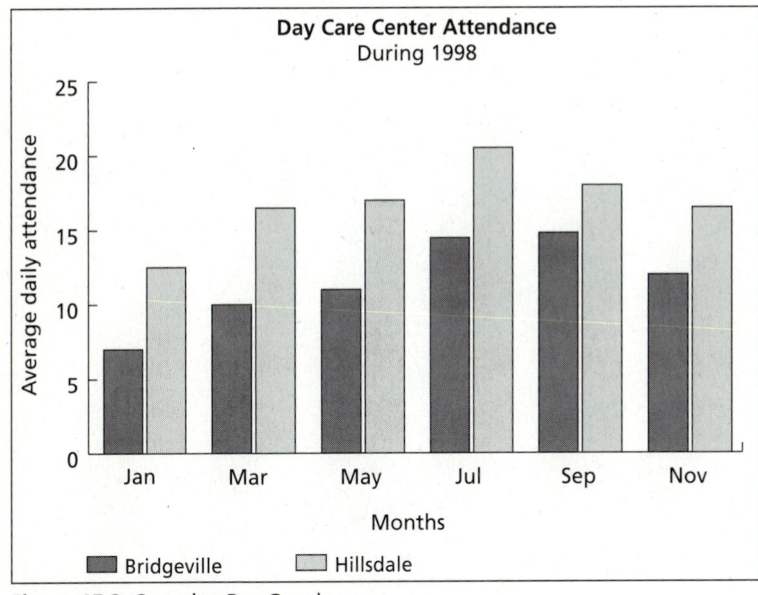

Figure 17.3 Complex Bar Graph

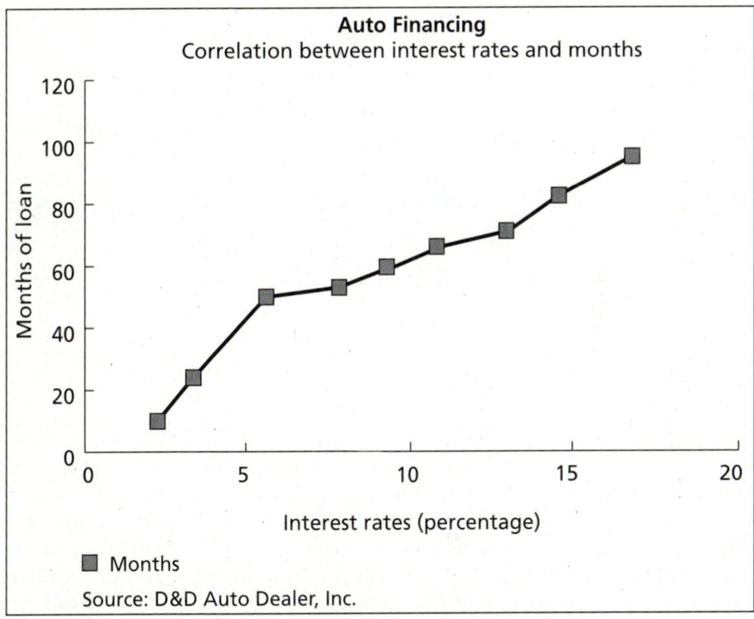

Figure 17.4 Correlational Line Graph

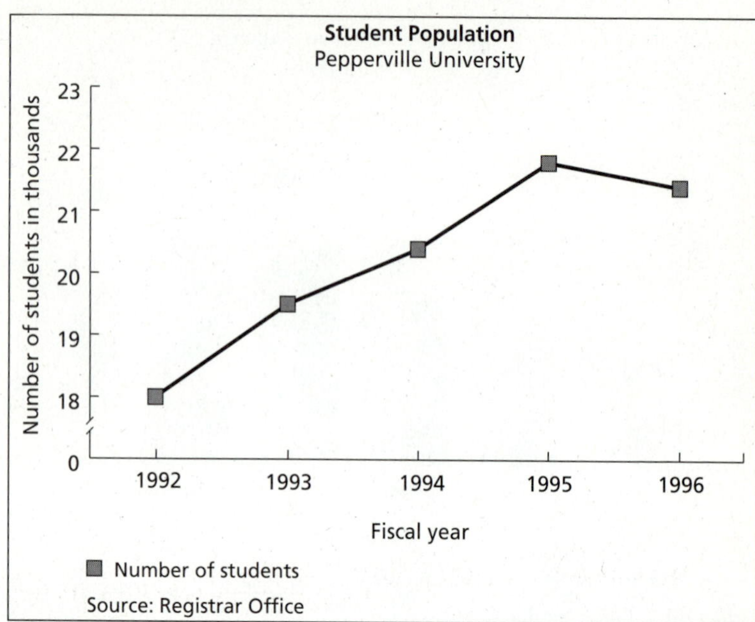

Figure 17.5 Line Graph with Fracture Signaling Irregular Initial Increment

When you construct graphs, be careful to indicate what quantities are being compared: dollars or millions of dollars, inches or miles. Clearly label both the X-axis and Y-axis and use an informative title above the graph. You can put labels elsewhere on the graph for clarity (note that the labels at the peaks of the bars in Figure 17.1 provide the exact values of each bar). Below the graph, credit the source of any data derived from information you have borrowed from outside your company or organization, as in Figures 17.4 and 17.5.

17.2 Dishonest Graphs

It is easy to distort information with a graph. Figure 17.6 depicts a correlational graph in which small increments (0.05, 0.1, and so on) set far apart along the Y-axis have been used to stretch the graph line upwards to give the impression of a large increase in revenues. That impression is accentuated by the crunching up of the X-axis. Figure 17.7 shows the same information graphed so as to provide a more honest representation of the data. As a writer, you judge what the data means and then accurately represent that meaning with the shape of your visual.

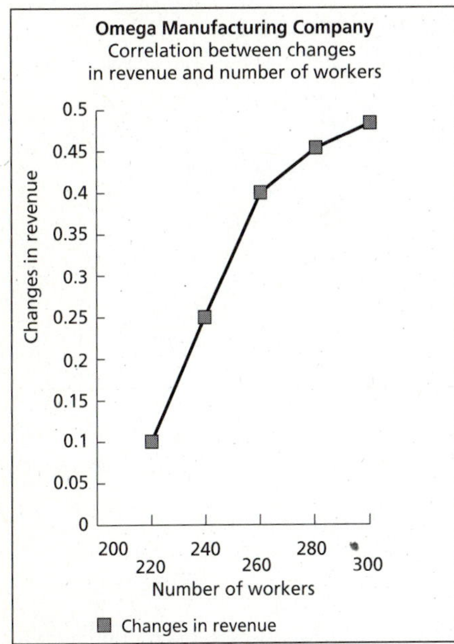

Figure 17.6 Dishonest Graph

17.3 Tables

Tables are useful for comparing items on the basis of many criteria. A table typically presents a vertical list of comparable items along the left edge of the graphic, with a set of criteria for comparison listed horizontally across the top or bottom. The data is placed in appropriate intersections in the resulting grid. Figure 17.8 provides an example.

17.4 Boxes

Boxes, also called "inserts," contain text that is not a part of the running text of the

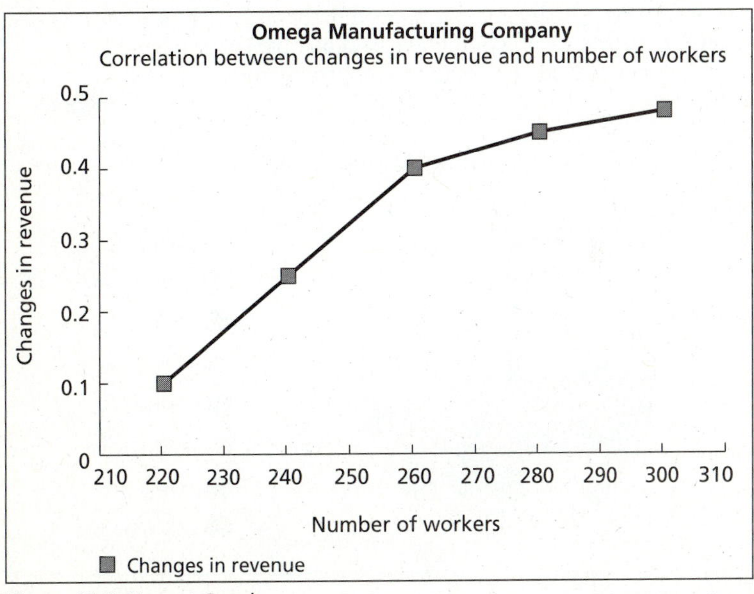

Figure 17.7 Honest Graph

Breakdown of Prices for Food and Nonfood Items

	Food				Non-Food			
	10 oz. Campbell's Tomato Soup	16 oz. Miracle Whip	14 oz. Wheaties	42 oz. Olde Fashioned Quaker Oats	Dial Gold Soap 3 pack	128 oz. Clorox	24 oz. Scope Mouth Wash	Hi-Dry Paper Towels
Family foods	.55	1.79	2.69	3.29	2.19	1.89	3.49	.79
Sunnyville Supermarket	.59	1.89	2.69	3.39	2.29	1.39	3.45	.73

Figure 17.8 Table

document. The boxes used throughout this textbook present model problems and solutions.

17.5 Charts

Two kinds of charts commonly appear in business reports: percentage charts and directional charts. Percentage charts show the breakdown of some quantity, such as yearly sales, into parts. Pie charts show the percentage of each part as a scaled, pie-shaped piece of a circle (Figure 17.9). Bar charts do the same thing but in a rectangular bar shape (Figure 17.10).

When you create percentage charts, the percentages must add up to 100 percent. That means, in a pie chart, you should allow 3.6 degrees of

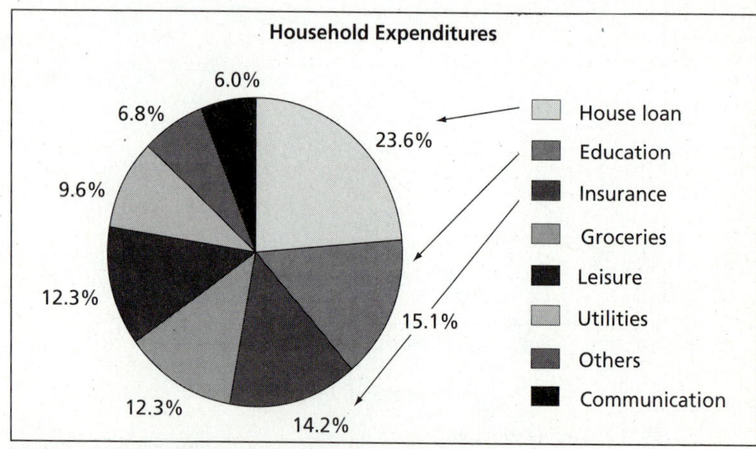

Figure 17.9 Pie Chart

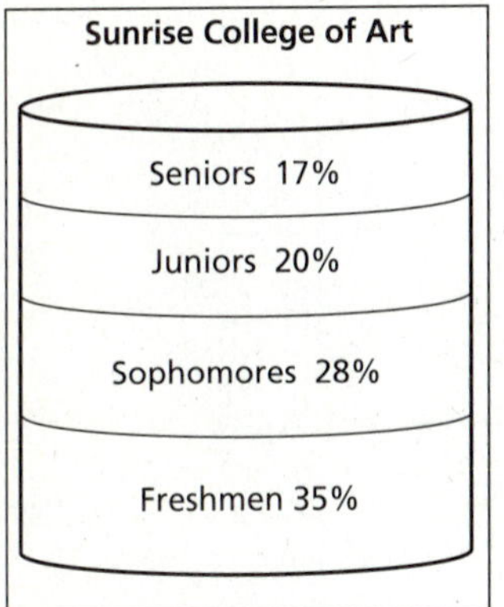

Figure 17.10 Bar Chart

the circle per percentage point. Moving from the top clockwise, place the largest pie segment first, the smallest last (see Figure 17.9).

Directional charts show the flow of something—the flow of authority in an organizational chart (Figure 17.11) or the flow of a procedure (Figure 17.12).

17.6 Referring to Visuals

Never put a graph, table, or chart in your document without mentioning it somewhere in your paragraphs of running text. Insert visuals as soon as possible after the first mention of them. When you construct graphs, put the word "Figure" plus a number in front of the title if there is more than one graph:

Figure 1 Comparison of Food Prices and Nonfood Prices

In the body of the text, you would refer to the above graph as "Figure 1." If your document contains only one graph, the title provides sufficient identification without the word Figure in front of it. In the body of your text, refer to the figure as "the graph":

As the graph shows, our store underprices our competitor in most hardware items.

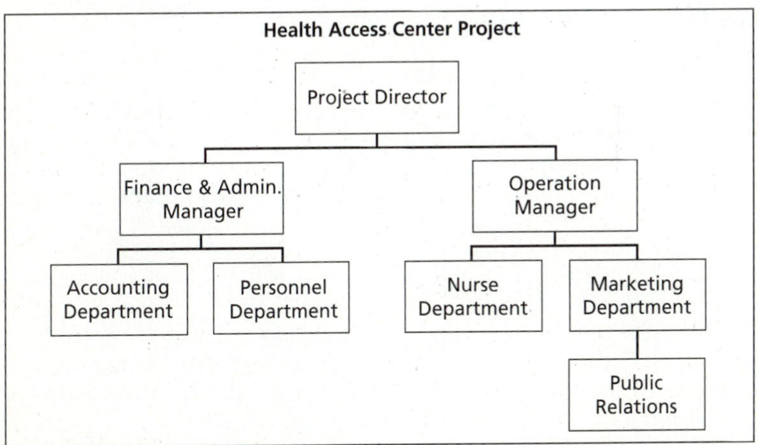

Figure 17.11 Organizational Chart

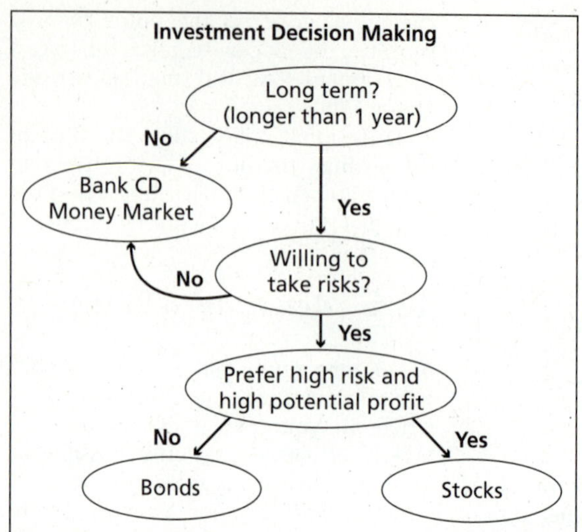

Figure 17.12 Flow Chart

Tables and charts are normally referred to as such (not as figures) and are numbered separately from figures:

> As Table 2 shows, our store underprices our competitor in. . . .
> As the pie chart indicates, costume jewelry accounted for. . . .

Problems for Classwork and Homework

P17.1 Find a Graph and a Table

Look through an issue or two of a business magazine, such as *Business Week* or *Fortune,* and find an interesting graph and an interesting table. Write a description of each. Explain why they struck you as interesting. Turn in both your description and a photocopy of the graph and table.

P17.2 Find a Box and a Chart

Look through a business magazine, such as *Business Week* or *Fortune,* and find an interesting insert (box) and an interesting chart. Write a description of each and explain why they struck you as interesting. Turn in both your description and a photocopy of the insert and chart.

P17.3 Bar Graph

Put the following information in a bar graph with an irregular initial increment on the Y-axis:

Student enrollment at Madison Junior College for 1997: 5,205
Student enrollment at Marsdale Technical College for 1997: 5,370
Student enrollment at Murrysburg College for 1997: 6,890

P17.4 Line Graph

Put the following information in a line graph with an irregular initial increment on the Y-axis:

Student enrollment at Rockville Junior College:

1960: 890
1970: 1,245
1980: 2,065
1990: 1,800.

P17.5 Complex Bar Graph

Put the following information about students' grades in a business writing class into a bar graph:

Male traditional students: Average Test Score: 78/Average quiz score: 86/Average Paper Grade: 82
Male Nontraditional students (26 years old or older): Average Test Score: 88/Average Quiz Score: 94/Average Paper Grade: 88
Female Traditional Students: Average Test Score: 87/Average Quiz Score: 90/Average Paper Grade: 86
Female Nontraditional students (26 years old or older): Average Test Score: 95/Average Quiz Score: 96/Average Paper Grade: 94

P17. 6 Correlational Line Graph

Put the following information in a correlational line graph. Include the years.

Percentage of nontraditional students (26 years old or older) at Pumpkinville College and the average GPA for all students:

4%/2.6 GPA (1980)
8%/2.8 GPA (1985)
15%/3.1 GPA (1990)
18%/3.3 GPA (1995).

P17.7 Table

Put the following information in a table:

EazyDo File Cabinets: Weight—22 lb.; height—4 ft.; width—3 ft.; depth—3 ft.; colors—gray only; price—$195.
Robins File Cabinets: Weight—38 lb.; height—4.5 ft.; width—4 ft.; depth—3 ft.; colors—brown, gray, white; price—$250.

P17.8 Pie Chart

Determine what percentage of your class fall into these age groups and then create a pie chart to represent those percentages: 18 and younger/ 19–20/21–25/26 and older.

P17.9 Bar Chart

Your company makes ice cream bars. Create a bar chart illustrating the breakdown of sales by flavor: chocolate: 45%; strawberry: 31%; orange: 18%; lime: 6%. If you're in a creative mood, you may shape the chart to look like an image of the product.

P17.10 Organizational Chart

Create an organizational chart of the academic administrators at your school down to the department-chair level.

P17.11 Flow Chart

Create a flow chart that illustrates the grade-appeal process at your school.

18

Short Report Based on Library Research

Libraries are not just for students. Professionals in the workplace obtain information in many different ways—by accessing internal files, by doing field research, by reading newspapers and trade journals, and by using public and university libraries. The assignments in this chapter ask you to write reports based on research using reference books and computer databases available in most academic libraries.

18.1 Report Format

Short internal research reports can be organized as memos with subheadings for every section after the introduction. You have a choice between two kinds of subheadings. You can use generic or standard headings, such as *Summary, Conclusions,* and *Recommendations,* which can be found in countless reports. Or you can create your own report-specific headings, such as *Advantages of Shipping Air Freight,* that are particular to the content of your report. It is common for report writers to use both types in the same report, mixing them together.

Headings can be centered or flush left, and in either position they can be in uppercase or lowercase. Following is the order of dominance, from the most general heading to the most specific:

CENTERED UPPERCASE
Centered Lowercase

FLUSH-LEFT UPPERCASE
Flush-Left Lowercase Note: Lowercase headings are often bold faced or underlined.

18.2 Library Resources

The most underrated resource in a library is the staff of librarians. Most librarians love to help people find the right book or article or piece of information. Take advantage of that. If you can't find what you need right away, ask a librarian for help.

Almost all college libraries and many public libraries use computerized indexes. These are useful for finding books and articles in magazines and professional journals. Learn your library's computer system, if you don't already know it. The library probably has a brochure showing the indexes available and how to get started.

Here are some important business-related reference books and computer resources, most of which are probably available in your school library:

Industry Information

1. Moody's Industrial Manual
2. Standard & Poor's Industry Surveys
3. U. S. Industrial Outlook
4. Almanac of Business and Industrial Financial Ratios
5. U. S. Global Trade Outlook 1995-2000
6. Encyclopedia of American Industries
7. F&S Index United States
8. Service Industries USA

Company Information

9. Moody's Handbook of Common Stocks
10. Standard & Poor's 500 Guide
11. Business Rankings Annual
12. Hoover's Handbook: Profiles of 500 Corporations
13. Hoover's Handbook of Emerging Companies
14. Hoover's Masterlist of America's Top 2500 Employers
15. National Directory of Women-Owned Business Firms
16. Findex: The Directory of Market Research Reports, Studies, and Surveys
17. Market Share Reporter
18. Moody's OTC Unlisted (small companies)
19. Mission Statements: A Guide to the Corporate and Nonprofit Sectors
20. Corporate Philosophies and Mission Statements: A Survey and Guide for Corporate Communicators and Management
21. Say It And Live It (mission statements)

Statistics

22. Statistical Abstract of the United States (U. S. Department of Commerce)
23. Datapedia of the United States 1790-2000 by George Thomas Kurian
24. Fedstats Web site at http://www.nemw.org/stats.htlm

General Computer Resources

25. Altavista, a World Wide Web search program: http://www.altavista.digital.com (see Chapter 27, section 27.3, for a list of search programs)
26. Yahoo's Business Database: http://www.yahoo.com/Business_and_Economics/companies
27. INFOTRAC General Business File (A computer database that will help you find articles in business magazines and journals)
28. EDGAR Database of Corporate Information: http://www.sec.gov/edgarhp.htm
29. Selected Business Resources on the Web: http://www.uwrf.edu/library/business.html
30. Pace University Business Library: http://library.pace.edu/electres.html#BUSINESS

Problems for Classwork and Homework

P18.1 Library Usefulness

The problems in the following exercises reveal the variety of ways in which library research can be useful in business. Read the problems and write a memo to your teacher suggesting two additional scenarios in which a business person would need to use a library to solve a problem.

P18.2 Industry and Company

Redo the model problem in Box 18.1, but select an industry reviewed by *Standard & Poor's Industry Surveys* other than the communications industry. Then select a company within your chosen industry that appears in *Moody's Handbook of Common Stocks*. After you finish your research, discuss your findings within your group, if you are working in groups. On your own, write up a report similar to the solution to the model problem in Box 18.2.

P18.3 Selective Investment

Your company has some extra cash that it needs to invest, and your boss, Roberta Roberts, has asked several teams to undertake research in order to select for investment or purchase either a small high-tech company or a small company known for its "social conscience."

Choose one of those two types of companies and use library and Internet sources to find an appropriate company. After your research is finished, discuss your findings within your group, if working in groups. On your own, write a persuasive memo report on your findings and recommendations.

Box 18.1

Model Problem: Short Report Based on Library Research

Your company has some extra cash that it needs to invest. Your boss, Roberta Roberts, has asked several teams to research certain companies and the industry they belong to. In addition, she wants a brief report making a recommendation about the industry in general and the company in particular as investment opportunities. Your group has been assigned one of the Bell spin-offs, SBC Communications. Do the research using Standard & Poor's Industry Surveys and Moody's Handbook of Common Stocks. Write the report based on your findings.

Introduction includes a statement of the problem and authorization.

Conclusion and recommendation

Paraphrased text is parenthetically documented with the author's name and the page number.

Because the same author is being cited, only the page number appears in the parenthetical note.

(Continued next page)

Box 18.2

Solution to Model Problem

TO: Roberta Roberts

FROM: Rick Susick, Jim Bailey, Larry Way, Lincoln Key

DATE: July 8, 19__

RE: Recommendation that we invest in SBC

Our company has approximately 1/2 million dollars in excess cash holdings at this time, and Vice President Roberta Roberts has assigned our research group the task of searching for a suitable investment opportunity within the communications industry.

On the basis of our research, we conclude that the communications industry is generally a good investment area. Within that industry, we recommend that our company invest a substantial portion of the available funds in SBC Communications, whose record over the past 10 years is impressive and whose approach to communications strikes us as exactly right for future growth and success.

THE COMMUNICATIONS INDUSTRY

Industry Record

The communications industry has been one of the most dynamic industries in the United States, thanks to recent state and federal deregulation, which has let the industry become highly competitive in the various telecommunication markets, such as telephone operating companies, interexchange carriers (long-distance carriers), wireless sevice companies, and telecommunications equipment and services (Gooley T16).

Not only are local and long-distance carriers competing with each other and with the cable television industry, they also face potential competition from providers of inexpensive Internet communications, used by "24 million people in the United States and Canada" (Gooley T16). Although the Internet is 5 to 20 times cheaper (depends on distance to a server), existing telephone operation enjoys superiority to the Internet in reliability, voice quality, immediacy of transmission, and especially capacity to handle large loads of traffic (T16).

As the cellular industry's rapid growth continues, wireless network systems may eventually replace the conventional landline network systems. Although the wireless network seems the way to go in the future, it may take some time because of technological difficulties in some applications and, more importantly, customers' resistance to changing from landline to wireless (T15).

Box 18.2 *continued*

Solution to Model Problem

Page numbering for a memo longer than one page

Roberta Roberts
July 8, 19__
Page 2 of 3

Some developing countries, such as China, are installing wireless network systems instead of conventional landline systems because of cost efficiency. The most rapid telecommunication growth is in the world's developing countries in Asia, Africa, Eastern Europe, and South America, where telephone communication is regarded as a luxury (T15).

Recommendation

The communications industry as a whole is likely to expand both domestically and internationally. We highly recommend investment in the communications industry. An individual company, in order to survive and succeed in the competitive market, must get into wireless networking and diversified services in the international market.

SBC COMMUNICATIONS

Company Record

The shortened title in the parenthetical reference ("SBC") connects the reader to the second entry in the Works Cited below. There's no page number because the source, Moody's, doesn't number its pages.

SBC Communications, Inc. (hereafter SBC), formerly Southwestern Bell, is a one of the "baby Bell" offspring of the breakup of AT&T in 1984. *Moody's Handbook of Common Stocks* lists SBC's operations as including a telephone operating company; mobile systems; wireless services and equipment in Europe, Latin America, South Africa, Asia, and Australia; business and consumer telecommunication equipment; messaging services; cable television intersects; and directory advertising and publishing ("SBC").

In addition, The New Telecommunications Act of 1996 enables SBC to provide long-distance service and to offer long-distance cellular services outside its five-state homebase of Texas, Missouri, Oklahoma, Kansas and Arkansas ("SBC").

Moody's reports that, in the past ten years, SBC's gross revenue, net income, and earnings per share have all increased every year. SBC outperformed all other former Bell companies in terms of total return of investment during 1995. Although there is no guarantee that SBC will continue to grow as rapidly as it has in the past five years, the company

Box 18.2 *continued*

Solution to Model Problem

Roberta Roberts
July 8, 19__
Page 3 of 3

seems to be on the right track with diversification of services, both domestically and internationally ("SBC").

In addition, *Moody's* says that SBC's price per earning ratio (P/E), which shows how high/low the stock is priced in terms of earnings per share, is not especially high compared with some popular stocks. During 1995, the industry as a whole had a P/E of about 15. SBC's P/E in 1995 was 15.8. Considering the good potential of SBC's future and steadily increasing dividends, the stock price is likely to go up this year ("SBC").

Recommmendation

We highly recommend SBC as a good, solid investment.

The timing of buying SBC's stocks may not be as crucial as when investing in small, growing companies. However, the market in general is currently regarded as over-priced and many economists expect a correction. Also, the Federal Reserve is likely to increase interest rates some time this year. Under such circumstances, we would recommend a conservative approach. Instead of investing the decided amount at one time, we should invest 20 percent of the amount monthly for five months so that the effects of purchase timing can be diversified.

Because it comes out weekly, *Standard & Poor's* is treated here as a magazine in the Works Cited. Entries in *Moody's Handbook* are most easily handled in MLA format as articles in a reference book. In business publications, these publications are sometimes treated as books.

Works Cited

Gooley, Kevin J. "An Industry in Transition." *Standard & Poor's Industry Surveys* 7 Dec. 1995: T15–T17.

"SBC Communication Inc." *Moody's Handbook of Common Stocks*. Spring ed. 1996.

P18.4 Finding Charities

You and your college roommate constitute a two-person financial-planning firm. One of your most important and wealthiest clients, Jane Weatherby, wants to increase her charitable donations and has asked you to prepare a list of possibilities for her. She is particularly interested, she says, in charitable and nonprofit organizations that help young people in trouble (pregnant teenagers, kids on drugs, and so forth). Use the library to put together an annotated list. Forward that list to Weatherby in a business letter. Invent addresses and letterhead stationery for your firm.

P18.5 Mission Statement

Henry Tuttle, the new president of your company, is dissatisfied with your organization's vague and lifeless mission statement. He has asked your group to research mission statements and submit a written report describing the conventions of these documents and some of the interesting options that show up in the mission statements of successful companies.

Use as many library and Internet sources as necessary to solve this problem. After your research is finished, discuss your findings within your group, if you are working in groups. On your own, write a memo report on your findings.

P18.6 The Mommy Track

As an employee of a chain of day-care centers, Kid Care, Inc., you have been asked to prepare a report on the feasibility of developing a two-track hiring system, one in which new female employees are groomed for full-time, life-long employment with unlimited advancement possibilities, and one in which new female employees would work only part-time with limited advancement possibilities, so that they could spend considerable time raising their own families.

This idea was controversial when it was first proposed. Research the "mommy track" idea and write a report that presents pros and cons, ending with a recommendation. Address the memo report to your supervisor, Janet Chang.

19

Short Report Based on Survey Research

Businesses and other organizations use surveys to ask people directly what they believe, prefer, or need in regard to products, services, and policies. Surveys often help businesses determine if customers are satisfied with products or services, or determine if a sufficient market exists to make a potential enterprise profitable.

Organizations survey people through in-person or phone interviews, or in writing, through questionnaires. Some mail the questionnaires or hand deliver them to respondents and either wait or return to collect them.

19.1 Problems with Surveys

In order to use surveys effectively, you need to understand their limitations and the problems inherent in their use. An ineffectively designed or delivered survey can produce misleading results.

19.1a Correctly Defining the Population

The **population** is the group of people whose views you want to know. If you inaccurately define the population, you will likely get a distorted picture. Suppose you were a college administrator who wanted to know what proportion of young entering freshmen at your university are having problems living apart from their parents for the first time. If you defined the population to be surveyed as the whole freshman class, your results would be inaccurate. Some first-year students are older and have been living on their own for some time. Also, some freshmen are still living at home and commuting. Your correct population would be those among the freshman class who are 17 or 18 years old, living in dorms or student apartments.

19.1b Getting a Representative Sample

When you survey a small group, getting representative opinions can be a direct process. For example, if you need the opinions of the people who work in your office, you ask everyone. However, most target populations are too big for that, so only a sample of the population is queried. It is important that the sample be representative of the whole population.

The first step in assuring a representative sample is to take a random sample, one in which each member of the population has an equal opportunity of being chosen. That is not always easy, and researchers often settle for something less than a perfectly random sample. For example, to obtain student opinion on an issue, a researcher might select every tenth name in the college's student phone directory to create a list of people to contact. Because some students have unlisted numbers, and others don't have phones, this method does not provide a perfectly random sample. Some members of the population have no chance of being selected. The researcher would have to evaluate the effect on survey results of not being able to access that portion of the population.

If your sample is too small, you run the risk of randomly selecting a nonrepresentative group. However, the larger your sample the more work and expense involved. For national studies, researchers might select about one thousand people; for regional studies anywhere from one hundred to seven hundred (Anderson, 1985).

You may want to analyze subgroups within your sample by taking a "stratified sample"; for instance, you might select an equal number of males and females from the overall population so that you can compare their responses. This, of course, does not produce a random sample of the whole population. Science proceeds by compromise.

19.1c Inaccurate Replies

Sometimes, out of shame or self-deception, people don't tell the truth when responding to questions. Their answers fail to represent their true feelings or situations. Respondents may also provide inaccurate answers if they don't understand the question. Survey questions must be carefully phrased for clarity. Pollster Richard Morin, for example, reports on a survey question which showed, erroneously, that 34 percent of Americans believed that the World War II Holocaust never happened. Respondents got confused by a double negative in the question: "Does it seem possible or does it seem impossible to you that the Nazi extermination of the Jews never happened?" (1997, p. 35).

Respondents sometimes shape their responses to fit what they believe the researcher wants to hear. Questions that encourage a particular response should be eliminated or revised. For example, the question, "Would you pay an exorbitant price for a gourmet pizza?" will almost certainly result in large number of "no" replies. The question should be revised: "Would you pay $15 for a sixteen-inch gourmet pizza baked in an authentic wood-fire oven?"

Avoid questions that call for difficult feats of memory ("How many times did you wash your car last summer?") If you need to ask such a question, offer the respondents a set of possibilities to choose from: 1-3, 4-8, more than 8.

19.2 Constructing the Survey

Your survey **instrument**, the questionnaire you develop, should be as short as possible, with the most interesting questions first, demographic questions last. The questions themselves fall into two general categories, closed and open. **Closed questions** offer the reader a choice of answers or ask for precise information: *"How many cars does your household own?"* **Open questions** ask the respondent to articulate a reply to a question that has no precise answer: *"What do you think characterizes a good restaurant?"*

The model survey in this chapter illustrates various types of questions, both closed and open. The variety of closed questions in the model is for purposes of illustration. A well-designed survey would use only one type, or at most only a few different types, of closed questions. It is common to ask both closed and open questions about the same subtopic.

Mailed questionnaires need a cover letter that explains the importance of the survey. Questionnaires that are handed to people and collected should also contain a brief statement at the top to introduce the survey and explain its purpose and importance.

19.3 Interviewing

Prepare an interview as you would a written questionnaire. List what you want to know, and then create a set of questions, closed and open, that you believe will elicit that information from the respondent. In interviews, you can ask follow-up questions, so monitor the responses to see if the respondent is giving you the information you want. If not, ask a follow-up question. Follow-up questions can also be used to explore unexpected, interesting revelations.

Begin the interview with a pleasantry in order to put the respondent at ease. Before asking the first question, explain the purpose and importance of the survey. Ask your respondent if he or she minds if you tape record the interview. Even if tape recording, take notes. Your notes constitute a summary of important points, and you will need them if the machinery breaks down. Keep the closed questions simple: "Did you eat pizza in the past month?" If necessary, use a follow-up question to clarify a response: "I need to put down an answer of yes or no. Shall I put that down as a yes?"

19.4 Analysis of Quantitative Data

Analysis of quantitative data is the conversion of **raw data** (the information you gathered in your research) into **central tendencies** (averages). When you present quantitative data in a report, you present the central tendencies, not the raw data. Raw data is usually too copious to be understood at a glance. There are three ways to average data, each one useful in its own way.

19.4a The Mean

The most familiar kind of average is the **mean**, which is calculated by summing all the responses and dividing by the number of responses. The following example is a scale question, such as might be used to compare the mean responses of graduate and undergraduate students:

4. _____ Where on this scale do you rate your university library?

1	2	3	4	5	6	7	8	9	10	11
|					|					|
Worthless					Adequate					Excellent

The summary of responses might look like this:

> The mean response from graduate students to this question was 4.9, 2.3 points lower than the 7.2 mean response from undergraduate students.

19.4b The Median

On some occasions you may wish to use another kind of averaging called the median. The **median** is the middle number in a range of numerical responses. If respondents give you the ages 17, 17, 17, 18, 19, 19, 19, and 56, the median age would be 18.5; there are four ages below it and four above it—it is the middle score. In this case, the median would give a better picture of the group than the mean, which is 22.8. Most of the members are teenagers, not people in their twenties. In fact, there are no twenty-year-olds in the group.

19.4c The Mode

The **mode** is the most frequent response given by the respondents. Determining the mode allows you to "quantify" textual responses. For example, if you ask college students this question:

What kinds of social events do you regularly attend?

you could identify the most common response, the mode, and report it:

> In response to the last question, 84 percent of the men mentioned "beer parties" or something synonymous, while only 15 percent mentioned high-culture events such as classical concerts or plays.

19.5 A Research Procedure

The following is a step-by-step procedure for developing and completing survey research projects.

1. List the basic questions you want answered. One basic question may result in any number of interview or written questions. For example, suppose you want to know how the lifestyles of male and female college students differ. You might break that down into lifestyle differences in academics, social life, and living conditions. To answer the third issue, living conditions, you might ask respondents where they live (dorm, apartment, home), how healthy a diet they maintain, whether they hold a job while attending classes, and so forth.
2. Carefully define the population. Write a description.
3. Determine how you will sample the population.
4. Develop your interview questions or written questions.
5. Conduct a pilot study, that is, test your survey instrument on a few members of the population. Look for flaws in your instrument (for example, questions that respondents don't understand or otherwise have difficulty answering, or questions that are misinterpreted or otherwise fail to elicit information you want).
6. If working in a group, divide up the labor and create a timetable for getting the work done.
7. Conduct your survey and, if working in a group, pool the raw data.
8. Study the data and do any averaging or counting that you need to do to get a sense of what your research has shown.
9. Write up the report.

19.6 Suggested Report Format

For a short internal report of the kind called for in the assignments in this chapter, you might use a memo format with subsections like those that appear below.

19.6a Introduction

Your introduction should answer these questions: ***When*** and ***why*** did ***who*** tell you to do ***what***? Identify the research question. For example:

> On May 28, 19--, Alex Weiss asked our marketing team to determine whether Pumpkinville, Ohio, would make a good location for a Gourmet Pizza franchise.

The introduction usually has no subheading and appears as a short piece of text below the memo heading. But the rest of the sections should have underlined, bold-faced, or upper-case subheadings. The subheadings can be centered or set flush-left (see Chapter 18, section 18.1, for a discussion of subheading format).

19.6b Procedure

Tell the story of your research. Indicate whom you surveyed and by what method. Refer to the appendix containing your survey instrument. Review step-by-step exactly what you and your group did to gather data. This section should be written in sufficient detail that another group could closely replicate your study. Make clear the extent and limitations of your information gathering.

19.6c Results

One effective way to present results is to create visuals and build your discussion around them. It is usually best to present the quantitative (numerical) data and the qualitative (non-numerical, verbal) data in reduced forms, such as totals or means or modes. Analyze the qualitative data, the answers to open survey questions, by looking for important trends. You may want to present a few responses as examples. Do not list all the responses.

Do not *comment* on the results in this section—all commentary goes in the next section. Present the facts without evaluation of them. Don't write, "A surprising 32 percent answered yes to this question." Write, "Thirty-two percent answered yes to this question." It is not necessary to review the responses to every question on your survey, but you should review all important outcomes in the results section, especially those that will contribute to your conclusions and recommendations. To introduce information about responses, you can use language like this:

> In response to a question on whether they were satisfied with the weekly movie selections, 54 percent of respondents said yes, 22 percent said no, and 24 percent said that they never went to the movies.

19.6d Conclusions and Recommendations

Your conclusions are an explanation of what the results mean in terms of the research question. Your recommendations are what you believe your organization should do in light of your conclusions.

19.6e Bibliography

List bibliographical entries for books, articles, or other works cited, if any, in the text.

19.6f Appendix

Include any documents or written instruments you used in the study. If you have only one appendix, do not number it. Simply call it Appendix and give it a title. If you have more than one appendix, number and title each one:

Appendix 2 Responses of Males

Problems for Classwork and Homework

P19.1 Campus Problem

In a small group, choose one of the topics below and create a questionnaire to poll the opinions of students. Determine the quality of your school's

a. Library and library services
b. Athletic facilities or competitive sports opportunities
c. On-campus living conditions (housing and food)
c. Social life on campus and in the community
d. Programs in your major
e. Faculty

After making up the questionnaire, conduct a pilot study by testing your questionnaire on your own group to determine any problems with your questions. Next, administer the survey to the whole class. Analyze the results and present the results orally to the class. Finally, turn in your own individual memo report on the study, addressed to an appropriate administrator or campus committee (invent one). Include a copy of the questionnaire in an appendix.

P19.2 Outside of Class

Do assignment P19.1, but administer the survey to students outside the class.

P19.3 Interviews

Do assignment P19.1, but interview students inside or outside of class, as your instructor prefers.

P19.4 Improve the University

The Campus Development Committee has issued a call for proposals for ideas to improve the university. Invent an interesting proposal for your campus or town. Some examples:

1. Turn the campus, or most of it, into a park accessible by foot and bicycle only; no automobiles, except maintenance vehicles.
2. Get rid of tenure for professors.
3. Have the university purchase houses in town and rent them to students, the profits going to. . . .
4. Develop a student publication that rates professors and courses.

Research your proposal in the library. Has any other campus or college town done this? Determine the popularity of your proposal by conducting a survey. Write up a report on your idea and your research for the Campus Development Committee.

P19.5 Off-Campus Survey

In a group, select an off-campus problem, or a problem that affects the town folk as well as students, and develop a survey instrument to determine the attitudes of nonstudent, town residents toward this problem and toward a possible solution.

Pilot test your instrument on five local citizens belonging to the target population. Develop a procedure for obtaining a representative sample and administer the survey to thirty members of the population. As a group, report your results to the class. Individually, write up a memo report for your instructor.

P19.6 Market Research

Invent a new business for your college town. Some ideas:

1. A new kind of restaurant (e.g., one serving Thai food)
2. A new kind of entertainment center (for example, a miniature golf course; a shooting range)
3. A three-screen drive-in movie theater
4. A new kind of clothing store (for example, used clothes or formal wear)

Plan and carry out survey-based market research on your idea to determine whether it would work. Write a memo report to your boss, Harriet Molson.

Box 19.1

Model Survey Illustrating Different Types of Survey Questions

Restaurant Preferences

Introduction explains the purpose of the survey and expresses appreciation for participating.

A group of investors is considering opening a restaurant in your town. The purpose of this survey is to determine what kind of restaurant would be most appreciated and most likely to succeed. Your views are highly valued. Thank you for participating in the survey.

Rank order question

1. Indicate your preference for restaurants by ranking each type. Put a 1 next to the restaurant you most prefer, a 2 next to your second favorite, and so on through 5, your least favorite.

___Fast food burger ___Pizza ___Italian ___Chinese ___Gourmet

Open question

2. What other types of restaurants do you like besides the ones listed above?

Lickert scale

3. ____By writing a number from 1 to 11 in the blank, indicate the likelihood that when going out to dinner you would choose to eat in a restaurant specializing in Italian cuisine.

1	2	3	4	5	6	7	8	9	10	11
Never happen					50-50					Certain

Check answers

4. Put a check mark next to each of these foods that you like a lot.

___ pizza ___ fried rice ___ steak
___ fish ___ shellfish ___ pasta
___ vegetables ___ fruit ___ sweet desserts

Yes/No–Either/Or

5. Do you believe that pizza is healthful or unhealthful food? Check one:

___ healthful ___ unhealthful ___ don't know

Open question

6. Describe the best meal—or one of the best meals—that you have eaten in a restaurant. Give as many details as you can remember, especially in regard to what made the meal so good. You may use the back of this form if you need to.

7. Your age: _____ Gender: _____ Home town: _______________

Fill-in-the-blank demographic questioning

20

Routine and Long Reports

Much of the important paper flow in an organization consists of short, routine reports. This chapter looks at several common types: product comparison, progress, incident, and trip. It also examines the structure of long reports.

20.1 Product Comparison Reports

Purchases within organizations usually require a product comparison to make sure that the right product is being purchased at the best price. Let's suppose your division's offices are going to be recarpeted. Your first step in purchasing carpet is to list the required features. Those features might be an appropriate color to match walls and window shades (light gray preferred); a high degree of sturdiness; a short pile, because office chairs must roll on it; a price of less than twelve dollars per square yard installed.

When you have a list of features, your next step is to create a table of information. Place the features along the top and list the products to be compared vertically at the left side of the table. Consult catalogs or communicate with sales personnel at the carpet outlets to gather information and fill in your table. Avoid technical terminology that might confuse someone who hasn't looked into the subject as deeply as you:

	Color Avail.	Sturdiness	Thinness (in.)	Price/ sq. yd.
McFee's	Lt. Gray	Very Strong	.25	11.50
Lassitur's	Lt. Gray	Strong	.50	10.25
Lewis's	Dark Gray	Strong	.75	10.00

On the basis of your information, make a decision about which product you will recommend. Also decide which other products meet enough of your requirements that they could be considered as alternatives. When you write your report, include the following organizational elements.

20.1a Executive Summary

An executive summary is a short section at the beginning of a report meant to be read by the decision maker. This may be the only part of the product comparison report your boss reads before signing off on the purchase, especially if the purchase is minor and your boss trusts your judgment. Format your report as a memo. Write the heading first, followed by a paragraph stating who authorized the purchase and when, and your recommendation.

20.1b Description of the Products

Begin with any products that are unacceptable. State why they are so. Move from the least desirable to the most desirable, ending with a description of the product you recommend. Describe the products in terms of how their features meet the requirements. Indicate which products could serve the purpose. Refer to the table as early in the section as possible.

20.1c Recommendation

You may decide that the most expensive product is the best buy because of its high quality and small price difference, or you may decide that another product is the better buy because it has adequate qualities and is much cheaper than the higher quality products. In this section, repeat your recommendation and present a line of reasoning to support it. Box 20.1 provides an example of a product comparison report.

20.2 Progress Reports

If you are engaged in a long project, your original timetable for completion will probably include submission of progress reports at specified intervals. These reports typically follow this organizational pattern:

- Where you stand in the overall project; whether or not you are on schedule
- A description of any problems that need to be addressed
- What your next steps will be

You should also include decisions that have been made, results, or any other information that your reader wants as early as possible. See Box 20.2 for an example of a progress report.

20.3 Incident Reports

Many companies require incident reports whenever a serious accident occurs, such as an unusual machinery breakdown, or any other unfortunate,

Box 20.1

Product Comparison Report

TO: Henry Mattison, Vice President
FROM: Rose Crane, Product Planning
DATE: September 4, 19__
SUBJECT: Comparison of carpets for Product Planning Division offices

On August 15, you asked me to compare carpets from local dealers to find the best carpet for the Product Planning offices. The situation required a color matching our walls and shades (preferably light gray); a strong, short pile (chairs must roll on it); and a price under $12.00 per square yard installed. After reviewing the qualities of the products available in the local stores (see the table on the next page), I recommend McFee's product.

Description of the Products

The carpet available at Lewis's is unacceptable. Although the dark gray might work, it would not look as good as the light gray offered by the other two stores. The main problem is that it is too thick for the kind of commercial use we will put it to. We need a nap no thicker than .5 inches.

The Lassitur carpet is acceptable, but inferior to the McFee carpet in strength. As the table shows, the McFee carpet has the best strength and the thinnest nap, making it the best product for our needs.

Recommendation

I recommend that we purchase the McFee carpet. Our offices require 540 square yards of carpet. At the prices indicated in the table, the cheaper Lassitur carpet would cost $5,536.00 to install, while the McFee carpet would cost $6,210.00, a difference of $674.00. Since we are installing carpet expected to last ten years, the price difference seems small when considering the advantages of strength and thinness that the McFee carpet offers.

Box 20.2

Progress Report

TO: Dean Millie Cragget
FROM: Dr. Sarah Neusenbaum, English Department
DATE: December 9, 19__
SUBJECT: Progress Report on Outcomes Assessment for Composition Program

In exchange for a one-class load reduction each semester for the next three semesters, I have assumed the responsibility of developing our department's plan for the state-mandated outcomes assessment of our composition program. My timetable calls for the completion of a plan for the first course in the program, ENG 100, by the end of this fall semester. That has been achieved. A copy of the plan is attached.

Problems

The plan has been submitted to the English department and has passed a vote of confidence, though not unanimously. Some English faculty have objected to the requirement that students include three drafts of each of the three essays in the portfolios they submit. These faculty want students to spend more time studying grammar and less time working on their papers. The outcomes-assessment plan, however, is consistent with our new composition program, which emphasizes writing and revision over the study of sentence errors outside the context of student writing. Outcomes assessment of a program must remain consistent with the program being assessed.

Next Steps

I have scheduled six meetings for the next semester, open to all English faculty, to discuss and develop a plan for ENG 101. In a memo to faculty, I have urged members who are concerned about the nature of outcomes assessment to attend these meetings and contribute to the debate while the program is being developed. I fully expect to meet the next deadline of May 7 for the ENG 101 plan.

unforeseen occurrence. First, you investigate the incident at the site, and then you write the report.

The report begins by answering the "journalist's questions": Who, What, Where, When, and How. Based on those answers, you make a judgment about fault, if any person or process is to blame. In the concluding section, you make recommendations about what your organization should do to avoid this problem in the future. See Box 20.3 for an example of an incident report.

20.4 Trip Reports

You may travel on company time and at company expense for many reasons besides making incident investigations. For example, you may travel to meet with customers or business partners, to examine or exhibit products at shows, or to attend educational conferences or workshops. For any such travel, you will probably be required to submit a trip report upon return. Your trip report communicates what you accomplished or learned to appropriate people in your organization.

Begin the report by describing when you traveled, where, and for what purposes. Provide details of what you learned that would interest your readers. You may have to include a record of your expenses. Conclude with recommendations, if appropriate. See Box 20.4 for an example of a trip report.

20.5 Long Reports

In general, a long report is one that requires a table of contents. Long projects lead to long reports. Such projects vary tremendously. You might find yourself writing a long report describing the feasibility of opening a branch office in Pumpkinville, Ohio; or the results of market research on a projected product; or the cultural and financial obstacles to entering a particular foreign market; or the need to diversify your product line to stay competitive; or the risks of expansion at this time.

When you undertake a long report within a one-semester college course, you should start the research part of the report early in the semester. Create a timetable for completion and stick to it. Your instructor may ask for progress reports. The following are sections typically found in long reports:

Transmittal Document

A cover letter or memo "handing over" the report. This short document (1) recounts the original authorization and purposes of the report,

Box 20.3

Incident Report

TO: Lon Sylvester, President, Green Hills Country Club
FROM: Wanda Wesinski, Manager
DATE: August 14, 19__
SUBJECT: Report on Dog in Shower Incident

On August 12, you asked me to look into the incident of a dog finding its way into the women's shower room at the club. I interviewed several club members who witnessed this occurrence. I also talked with club member Margaret Peach, who suffered a minor injury in the incident.

What Happened

On August 11, at 1:00 PM, a huge dog with no collar found its way into the women's shower room, startling two women in the showers, one of whom fell and injured her elbow. The injured woman was Margaret Peach, age 61. Ms. Peach was taken to the Brookville Clinic, where Dr. Pierce gave her a pain killer and examined her arm. Ms. Peach assured me she sustained no serious damage.

The dog escaped and hasn't been seen since.

Recommended Action

The club should pay Ms. Peach's hospital bill of $42.00.

I have notified the town authorities about the collarless dog. I will follow up to make sure that they are diligently searching for this animal.

The dog was able to enter the porch area of the club by pushing on the screen door at the end of the porch. I recommend that this door be refit to open outward. The dog got into the women's locker room because the door from the hall is often left partly open to vent steam. I recommend a fan to solve that problem so that the door can remain fully closed at all times.

Box 20.4

Trip Report

TO: Pumpkinville School Board
FROM: Arnold Pringle, Superintendent, Pumpkinville Area Schools
DATE: June 30, 19__
SUBJECT: Conference Session on Zero Tolerance

On July 20th I traveled to Frostburg, MD, to attend a day-long conference on student misbehavior in schools. A full record of my expenses is attached. In summary, the trip cost $345.80.

Purpose of the Trip

My main purpose was to attend the three-hour morning session on zero-tolerance policies. We have discussed expanding our zero-tolerance policies to drugs and sexual harassment. I found the session quite relevant to our concerns.

Support for Zero Tolerance

The federal Gun-Free Schools Act of 1994 requires us to have a zero-tolerance policy on guns in school. Violators must be expelled. This has worked well at Pumpkinville. It has also worked at other schools nationwide, according to the session leaders. The problem is toy guns. Several students around the country have been suspended for bringing plastic toys to school, most notably a case in Seattle in which a ten-year-old boy was suspended for bringing to school a one-inch plastic accessory to a G. I. Joe doll. The press ridiculed school officials for this action. The session leaders offered these justifications for zero tolerance for toys: (1) guns are getting smaller, and (2) police have shot children who were waving gun-like objects.

Keys for Implementing Zero Tolerance

The session leaders advised the following for implementation of zero tolerance for guns, drugs, and sexual harassment:

1) Involve the community in deciding what will be banned absolutely.
2) Allow yourself some flexibility in punishment.
3) Have an appeal process for students.
4) Train your staff.

Recommendations

The session convinced me that zero tolerance is an effective policy if done right. As a first step, I recommend that the board schedule a public hearing to inform local citizens of our interest in expanding zero tolerance to other areas and to get their feedback.

(2) mentions any changes in those purposes that occurred during the work of the project, (3) remarks on the outcome of the project, and (4) thanks those outside the project team who helped.

Title Page

Your organization may have a form for the title page. If not, include (1) the title, (2) who is submitting the report, (3) the organization affiliation of the report writers, (4) to whom the report is being submitted, and (5) the date of submission (month and year).

Table of Contents

List the chapter or section titles with page numbers. You may also list sub headings with page numbers. Pages before the first page in the body are traditionally numbered with lowercase Roman numerals.

Lists of Figures, Tables, Boxes, and Exhibits

Provide a separate List of Figures, List of Tables, and so forth for every kind of visual you employ. Report writers sometimes refer to any kind of visual as an exhibit. This term allows flexibility, but make sure that the terminology used in each list matches that used in the report. Provide page numbers.

Preface

The preface is an informal statement by the author(s) very similar to a transmittal document. Although the transmittal letter or memo may not be filed permanently with the report, the preface remains part of the report for its lifetime.

Forward

The forward is an introduction written by someone other than the report author(s). The forward usually praises the writer(s) and the report, points out the significance of the report's findings, and supports the report's recommendations.

Executive Summary

The executive summary is a short, typically one-page summary written for the decision maker. (Book-length reports may have much longer executive summaries.) The summary is designed for top executives who haven't the time to read long reports searching for advice on what action they should take. Follow this organizational plan: (1) Begin with a statement of the problem, (2) present important findings in the order in which they appear in the report (but omit detailed information or extended arguments; decision makers will read other parts of the report if they want to know more), and (3) state your recommendations.

Introduction

Include in the introduction the purpose of the report and the problems it examines. You may also describe the organization of the report.

Body of the Report

Section 20.6 describes ways of organizing the body of a long report.

Appendices

Include in the appendix or appendices (1) important research instruments, such as surveys, (2) important raw data (or samples of that data), (3) additional graphs and tables of detailed information, and (4) if possible, documents written by others to which you refer in your report.

Bibliography

Index

An index is necessary only for very long reports.

20.6 Organizing the Body of a Long Report

One of the most common approaches to organizing any document is the problem-solution approach. Box 20.5 presents a typical organizational pattern based on problem-solution.

Another common organizational pattern is the scientific format (Box 20.6). This is especially useful for research studies designed to test an **hypothesis** (for example, "Our competitors are not underpricing us, despite the rumors").

The above two represent generic approaches. You can always personalize your report headings to make them fit your specific subject matter. For example, in Box 20.5, the first section is called Background to the Problem. A personalized heading might read: "The Failure of Our Discount Program to Increase Sales."

In the end, you should arrange your subject matter in blocks and present those blocks in an order that your common sense tells you will be convenient for your audience and effective for your purpose. Some general advice:

- Orient the reader at the beginning by revealing your purposes and your organization.

Box 20.5

Problem–Solution Report Organization

1. Background to Problem

   --Where the problem occurs

   --Causes

   --Consequences

2. False Solutions

   --Solutions that have failed, and why

   --Solutions that might be anticipated but will fail, and why

3. Your Solution
4. Why Your Solution Will Work
5. Plan for Implementation

Box 20.6

Scientific Report Organization

1. Introduction/May Include a Review of Other Studies
2. Procedures

   --Instruments used

   --Description of human subjects, if any

   --What you did to gather information
3. Results

   --Quantification of information

   --Report on qualitative (nonnumerical) information
4. Conclusions

   --Interpretation of results

   --Recommendations for action or further study

- Avoid bringing in ideas that require a familiarity with material that doesn't appear until later in the text.
- Provide the basis for your conclusions and recommendations in the middle sections, so that they are convincing when you finally state them.
- Explain the significance of data as you go along; don't just dump facts on the reader's head.
- Make sure that your recommendations follow logically from your data and your conclusions.

Box 20.7, "Organization of a Marketing Plan," provides a sample structural design for one kind of long report.

Problems for Classwork and Homework

P20.1 Office Equipment

Your office has outgrown one of these items: filing cabinets, L-shaped secretarial desks, desktop computers used for word processing and database management, answering machines, or an item of your own selection. Your boss, Len Zuberkoski, has asked you to do the necessary research on this piece of office equipment and present him with a product comparison report and recommendation for a purchase.

Write a report that compares three brands by four to eight important characteristics, including price. Use catalogues, visit stores, talk to secretaries—whatever you have to do—to obtain your data. For your report, create a table and refer to it early in the report.

P20.2 Progress on Marketing Project

Examine the marketing report plan in Box 20.7. Assume that you have completed your analysis of the "Current Market Situation." Write a progress report, inventing details. To select a product or service being investigated, refer to Chapter 22 and select an entry from the list in exercise P22.4.

P20.3 Robbery Incident

You are a district manager for Simons Oil. During a late-night robbery at one of your service stations an armed thief stole more than four hundred dollars. This makes no sense; your night-shift employees are supposed to keep no more than one hundred dollars in cash in the register. As additional cash comes in, they are to deposit it into a tank safe, which cannot be opened until you come by the next day with the key. Your boss at headquarters, Herb Mantel, has asked you to investigate and submit an incident report. Do so, inventing details.

Box 20.7

Organization of a Marketing Plan

EXECUTIVE SUMMARY

CURRENT MARKET SITUATION

- Need
- Competition

OPPORTUNITY AND ISSUE ANALYSIS

- Product strengths
- Product weaknesses
- Opportunities
- Risks
- Issues

OBJECTIVES

MARKET STRATEGIES

- Positioning
- Product line
- Pricing
- Distribution outlets
- Advertising and Promotion

ACTION PROGRAMS

PROJECTED PROFIT–LOSS ANALYSIS

CONTROL

- Monitoring
- Progress Report Schedule

P20.4 Trade Show Trip

Examine the list of products in P22.4 (Chapter 22) and select one that you would enjoy demonstrating at a national trade show in Miami. Assume that you were sent by your company to the Miami show to demonstrate your product and look for possible distributors. Write a trip report, inventing details.

P20.5 Long-Report Ideas

Here is a list of research questions on which to base a long report:

a. How do local business people and English instructors at your school differ in their views as to what constitutes good writing? You can begin with library research and do some survey research.
c. Identify a particularly successful academic or nonacademic program at your school. Find out why it is so successful. Describe the program, its history, and the reasons for its success.
d. Report on the job market in your area. Examine the classified sections of newspapers, interview local business people, and use other sources. Who's getting hired to do what?
e. Of the major companies that existed at the turn of the twentieth century, few have survived to the close of the century. Determine what characteristics the survivors have in common.
f. Determine who are the five best instructors at your school.
g. Determine whether unionism is on the rise or in decline in your area.

21 Proposals

Proposals are offers to do work, to provide a product, or to initiate a project. You submit an internal proposal to your supervisor when you have an idea for improving the organization. External proposals go to people outside your organization. When you send a proposal in response to another organization's request for proposals (RFP), yours is a "solicited" proposal. If you submit a proposal to an external organization that hasn't asked for one, you submit an "unsolicited" proposal.

All proposals are persuasive documents. When you write such a document you argue in favor of your services or products at every opportunity.

21.1 Internal Proposals

An effective employee is always on the lookout for valid ways to improve operations, save money, and in general solve problems within the organization. When you come up with an idea that would benefit your organization, you may choose to pass it on to your supervisor through a written proposal. Even if you run the idea by your supervisor orally, you may be asked to "put it in writing."

In large organizations, major projects typically begin with a written proposal and end with a written report, with progress reports in between. In this way, all work is documented.

Use a problem-solution organizational structure for an internal proposal (see Box 20.5 in chapter 20). Boxes 21.1 and 21.2 display a model problem and a solution for an internal proposal.

21.2 Solicited External Proposals

When an organization wants to purchase products or services that it cannot provide itself, it sends out **requests for proposals** (RFPs) to companies likely to be interested and competent, to solicit competitive bids on the project. Sometimes the RFP is publicly advertised.

If you are a potential product or service provider, you will need to study the RFP first to decide whether or not to make a bid, and second to plan the contents of your proposal if you decide to go forward. The RFP may tell you the exact format your proposal must follow and what information you must include. If you fail to follow such instructions, you will probably be eliminated from the competition. Pay close attention to the due date. Late submissions are usually ineligible for consideration.

Solicited proposals follow a standard organizational pattern. Adjust that structure only in response to particular requirements specified in the RFP, if any. Otherwise, follow the structure described below:

Introduction

Introduces the document, explaining that it is a response to a specific RFP.

Background to the Problem

Describes the situation and the problem or need. Of course, the readers already know the nature of their own problem—this section shows that *you* understand it, too. You may include a new slant on the problem that the readers haven't thought of.

Proposed Plan

Explains how you will solve the problem. If the RFP requests consulting, you would explain here how you would go about studying and analyzing the part of the soliciting company's operations that require change. If the RFP calls for the development and manufacture of a product, you would provide in this section a production plan. If the RFP asks for the installation of computers, electrical wiring, wallpaper, or some other improvement to the facilities, you would indicate how you would do the installation and, if appropriate, how you would train personnel to use new equipment that you installed.

If this large section runs several pages, you can divide it up under subheads: Procedure, Budget, Personnel. The procedure section describes your proposed actions and provides a timetable for completion of the work. The budget section describes your charges and how they break down. The personnel section describes the people who will be working on the project and their qualifications (professional vitae are often provided in an appendix). Use every opportunity in this section to stress the quality of your personnel and their work, and to make clear the superior features of any materials you are selling or installing.

Conclusion

Presents a persuasive argument for selecting your company for the job. In this section you describe your competence. Your ideas and competence count, because contracts are not always automatically awarded to the

Box 21.1

Model Problem: Internal Proposal

You are the manager of a Bingo Store, part of a supermarket chain. Convince your boss, Regional Manager Amanda Stern, of the wisdom of your idea via a memo proposal. Here are the details:

- Business has been slipping on a regional level.
- To dramatically increase sales, you wish to propose a "Frequent Shopper Program" that will give free groceries twice a year to people who buy more than a certain amount during each six month period. The more they buy above the minimum amount, the more they get.
- This scheme would require issuing cards to customers that could be read by the computer in your cash registers, or by some other device at the checkout counter, to keep a record of each customer's purchases.
- You could also use the data to determine food preferences and then send out ads for sales on products to appropriate sets of customers, for example, Pepsi ads to customers who buy Pepsi.
- Suppliers might chip in on the cost of the free food payoffs in exchange for a mailing list of people who buy their products.
- Risk can be reduced by starting with a pilot study at your store.

Statement of the problem

A false solution is mentioned

Reminder that this is not just the writer's problem, but also the reader's problem

Statement of the recommended solution

Why the solution will work

How the solution would be implemented, and more detail in support of the solution

Action statement: what the writer wants the reader to do

Box 21.2

Solution to Model Problem: Internal Proposal

TO: Amanda Stern, District Manager
FROM: Jerry Powell, Manager, Coaltown Bingo store
DATE: June 5, 19__

SUBJECT: A proposal to increase sales through a Frequent Shopper Program

BACKGROUND: DECLINING SALES

For the past year, sales have been declining in our region. This negative trend has affected every store, including mine in Coaltown. Our regional effort to counter this decline, although well conceived, has not been successful. Our coupon mailings have not brought in new customers, nor, apparently, have they increased shopping from our old customers.

It is time to try something new. None of us want the profits in this region to fall any further.

NEW SOLUTION: A FREQUENT SHOPPER PROGRAM

I wish to propose a Frequent Shopper Program to increase sales. Twice a year, frequent shoppers who purchase a minimum dollar amount would be rewarded with certificates for free groceries in our stores. The size of each certificate would vary according to how much the shopper exceeded the minimum needed to qualify.

This program should encourage infrequent shoppers to come to our store to try to meet the minimum, and it should work to retain the loyalty of our regular shoppers, possibly even encouraging them to buy more.

OTHER BENEFITS

I suggest giving free T-shirts to those who qualify for free groceries with the slogan "I'm a Frequent Shopper/At Bingo." This would provide our stores with free advertising.

The cards we would issue to keep track of customer purchase totals could also keep track of who buys which products and aid in creating mailing lists, which we could use to selectively advertise sales. We might also be able to sell those lists to vendors.

PILOT STUDY

To reduce the risk of this venture, I would be willing to conduct a pilot study at my Coaltown store. That way, if the project fails, regional profits would be affected only slightly.

If this idea appeals to you, let's have a meeting to discuss it.

lowest bidder. If possible, refer to other similar work you have done, or to satisfied clients who have agreed to answer questions and speak on your behalf to prospective customers. See Boxes 21.3 and 21.4.

21.3 Unsolicited External Proposals

Unsolicited external proposals require more salesmanship. The potential customer may not yet know—or yet believe—that his or her organization has a problem or need. Your first job, then, is to demonstrate the existence of that problem. In the opening paragraph or two of your proposal letter you must explain how you know that the reader has, or may have, a problem or need, and state how you will help.

Following that opening, present a proposal similar to the solicited proposal described above. Explain what you will do for the potential customer. You may not be able to provide a precise budget, but give the reader the closest estimate you can. As part of your proposal, you can offer to make a free estimate of cost. Discuss your competence and refer to satisfied customers. Boxes 21.5 and 21.6 illustrate an unsolicited proposal.

Problems for Classwork and Homework

P21.1 Choose an Internal Problem

Choose a real problem at your school. Invent a solution and write an internal proposal to the University Strategic Planning Committee. Here are some ideas to get your mind working: inadequate student parking; losing athletic teams; bad air circulation in a classroom building; inadequate food services on campus; poor scheduling of courses; weak advisement system; too few senior faculty teaching basic courses; out-of-control Student Association fees.

P21.2 Research Policy Proposal

Your small college just hired a psychology professor, Dr. Susan Yakitori, because of her strong research record in animal behavior. Your college president, Dr. Ralph Stone, hopes that Yakitori will inspire students and other faculty to pursue more original research.

As a newly hired assistant to the president, you support his goal. However, after hearing about an incident in which a chicken met a painful death in Yakitori's lab, as part of an experiment, you decide to look into the situation. You discover that the experiment was not a part of any original research, but merely a demonstration of methods of research. You also learn that your institution does not have a policy for approving and monitoring human and animal subject research.

Write a memo to President Stone proposing such a policy. Show the need for the policy, outline its contents, and indicate how it can be written and put into effect. Remember, Stone hired Yakitori, and he strongly supports her kind of research.

P21.3 RFP and Response

Write an RFP and a responding solicited proposal for one of the items below. Follow the models in Boxes 21.3 and 21.4.

a. A new computer for the secretary-bookkeeper of a hardware store.
b. Bathroom floor tiles (you may substitute front door locks, kitchen cabinets, carpeting, or some other item) for a new ten-unit apartment building.
c. Two tennis courts (you may substitute basketball courts, a walking path, twelve benches, or some other enhancement) for a town park.

P21.4 Read Master

You are the president of Read Master, a small consulting firm that trains business executives and employees to increase their reading speed without losing retention. You do not peddle gimmicks or make outrageous claims. You guarantee an average 20 percent increase in the number of words read per minute, and you project increases of closer to 30 percent for most trainees. You also teach the Greek and Latinate word roots and affixes that permeate the English vocabulary, so that readers will not have to turn so often to a dictionary. Write an unsolicited proposal to a company in your area offering your services.

Box 21.3

Model Problem: Soliciting Proposals

Purchasing Office (828) 311-9878
Pumpkinville College FAX: (828) 121-9888
Pumpkinville, OH 34456

Request for Proposals

Product or Service Description

Pumpkinville College seeks proposals for the purchase and installation of a copying machine for the Journalism Department. The machine should be able to (1) print heavy volume, (2) print pages from thick books, (3) print quickly, and (4) print on both sides of the page. We expect a three-year on-site warranty. Total price not to exceed $1,400.

Also required: (1) Instruction for secretary in the Journalism Department and (2) provision of a telephone or e-mail hotline for questions.

Delivery Schedule and Conditions

Delivery and installation before March 3rd, 19__. We take possession after installation and testing.

Payment Terms

Net 30 days.

Deadline for Bids

Bids must arrive by close of work day on February 10, 19__. Bid opening the morning of February 11. Notification by February 14, 19__.

Box 21.4

Solution to Model Problem: Solicited Proposal

Joe's Office Equipment
785 Bird Street
Pumpkinville, OH 34456

This is a proposal to provide the Journalism Department with a photocopier that will meet the department's needs at a price lower than that offered by the chain office supply stores. We recommend the Kanox CX 2400 Fast Feeder copier at $1,045.

THE KANOX CX 2400 MEETS YOUR DEPARTMENT'S NEEDS

The Journalism Department needs a fast, heavy duty printer that can print on both sides. You also need a printer designed to handle thick books, such as those used in libraries.

The Kanox CX 2400 provides these relevant features:

- 24 copies per minute
- Instant warm up
- Two 500-sheet paper drawers
- Legal-size paper in either drawer
- Reduces and enlarges in 1% increments, from 70% to 141%
- Standard automatic duplexing
- Photo/Book/Toner Saver modes
- Auto shut off
- Rated heavy duty

INSTALLATION AND TRAINING

Price includes installation and training within one week of receiving the order. On the day of installation, our training specialist will spend one hour with the Journalism secretary providing instruction in this easy-to-use machine.

In addition to the company documentation, we provide our own four-page simplified documentation for operation and basic maintenance. You may call us at our store at any time for help. If necessary, our trainer will return to your premises to help your secretary understand the operation of the copier.

The Kanox CX 2400 comes with a three-year on-site full warranty, parts and labor, with various warranty extensions possible. We include a toner cartridge, a ream of paper, and a cleaner.

We have installed two of the Kanox CX 2400s at Baylor Junior College in administration offices. The secretaries there are pleased with the machine and our service and will be glad to testify to that.

Box 21.5

Model Problem: Unsolicited Proposal

You are a small roofing contractor always on the lookout for new jobs. On a street in the historic section of your town are four late-nineteenth-century brick houses of the same design. Three have contemporary shingles on their roofs, including one that you did, and one has the original slate shingles. Two days after a big rainstorm you happen to be driving by and you notice a workman on the slate roof making a repair. You suspect that the slate roof leaks regularly. By asking around, you find out that the slate-roofed home is owned by George Munchin, a retired bank executive. You decide to mail Munchin an unsolicited proposal to end his leaks permanently by replacing his slate shingles with modern shingles.

Argument that a problem exists

Plan for solving the problem

Estimated cost

Description of personnel

References

Timetable for completion of the job

Box 21.6

Solution to Model Problem: Unsolicited Proposal

UNIVERSAL ROOFING
(412) 785-5555

Dear Mr. Munchin:

Driving by your house the other day I noticed a worker fixing your slate roof. I am familiar with houses like yours. In fact, I replaced the roof on the same model down the street, Mr. Clancey's home. Are you having the same problem that Mr. Clancey was having — small but persistent leaks after almost every big rain? Eventually, small leaks will begin to seriously damage the wood under the shingles, as well as the ceilings and walls inside your home.

What We Can Do for You

My company will end your leakage problem for good by replacing your slate roof with Owens Corning Supreme twenty-five-year shingles and #30 felt paper, and by providing new metal on chimneys and a drip edge. We will replace any bad wood. Price includes front porch and garage and your choice on color of shingle. We will haul away all the old shingles and clean up perfectly.

Until I can measure your roof and examine the wood underneath, I cannot give you an exact price, but at this time I would estimate that the charge to you will be about $4,000.

Our roofers are permanent employees, all of whom have been with us more than ten years. We are roofing specialists; we do no other kind of construction work. If you wish to talk with Mr. Clancey about the job we did on his house, he will be happy to talk to you. His number is 785-0022. You may be able to find someone who will underbid us slightly, but you won't find anyone who will provide you with better quality materials and craftsmanship.

Terms

We are busy, but we will be on site within 30 days of signing a contract, and we will work steadily until the job is finished. It shouldn't take more than one work week. Before purchasing materials, we require a down payment of 50 percent of the cost of the job.

Please call me in the evenings if you have any questions.

—John Blackstone, President, Universal Roofing

22

Sales Letters

A sales letter is a persuasive message sent to potential customers to ask them to try out your product or service. Organizations also send such letters to existing customers or contributors to maintain their loyalty and interest, and to past customers or contributors to try to win them back.

22.1 Possibilities for the Beginning

Many people automatically toss away sales letters without reading them. To avoid this, create a beginning section that will grab the reader's attention and interest. You may have only a second or two to succeed. Begin with a statement about your product or service or about the reader's needs that will make the reader want to continue reading. You may choose to highlight your attention grabber by setting it off dramatically (see Boxes 22.1 and 22.2).

22.2 Possibilities for the Middle

The middle of your sales letter should promote your product or service and showcase its worth. Dispel any worries or objections that might occur to readers. For example, the middle section of the model sales letter in Box 22.1 reads in part:

> Monster Pitter has the size and strength to handle *any* olive. And it has the delicacy to pit the smallest olive without splitting the flesh.

The first sentence showcases the instrument's power. The second sentence dispels concern that this hefty tool may be too crude for delicate jobs.

Box 22.1

Product Sales Letter

TOTAL KITCHEN

your complete kitchen supplier

March 15, 19__

My olive pitter doesn't work!

That's what our customers keep telling us. The olive pitters on the market today are too small to handle the big Calamata, Sicilian, and Spanish olives we all love to cook with. And they mangle the small cocktail olives!

INTRODUCING . . .

Monster Pitter

Just $19.50 with discount

Monster Pitter has the size and strength to handle *any* olive! And it has the delicacy to pit the smallest olive without splitting the flesh.

We developed this product just for home kitchen chefs like you. Now you can serve your favorite olives in a pasta dish or on an hors d'oeuvre plate without worrying about your guests cracking their teeth on a pit, or without ruining the appearance of the olives by having to slice them to remove the pit.

Send in the attached discount sticker with your order to get our introductory $2.00 discount. Act now! The discount is good only through May, 19__.

Box 22.2

Request-for-Donation Sales Letter

Elk Hollow Public Library

R.D. 6
Elk Hollow, PA 15410
(412) 767-4585

March 28, 19__

Dear Friend of the Library:

A MAJOR LIBRARY PROGRAM IS SINKING — WE'RE REACHING FOR YOUR HAND!

Your support has made a difference in the past, and it can do so again. Thanks to you and other regular contributors, we now bring in all the new bestsellers as soon as they make the *New York Times* list. We have adult reading classes. And we have a reading program for children.

Unfortunately, the children's program is at risk!

Our reading instructor, Mary Buckelew, who was doing this work for no pay, has had to retire for health reasons. We have not been able to find a volunteer with the appropriate background in reading instruction to replace Mary, and we are going to have to hire someone — or let the program drop!

In addition to your regular contribution of $50, we are asking for an additional $50 this year to specifically finance the children's reading program. Last year, this program:

- Helped fourteen children with reading difficulties improve two or more grade levels
- Helped five nonreaders get started on the road to reading

As you know, a child who is significantly behind in reading skills will almost certainly fail in school. These are the children of our own small community, and we don't want any of them to become losers when it comes to education.

Please fill out the enclosed information card and send your check for $100 made out to the Elk Hollow Public Library. The children and I thank you.

--Louise Bellsworth, Library Director

22.3 Possibilities for the End

Conclude your sales letter by telling your readers what you will do for them and what you want them to do. For example:

> To get a month's free sample, fill in the enclosed card and mail it before July 1.

22.4 Content Limitations

Don't address your pitch to the whole world. Consider who your likely clients are and focus on what will appeal to them.

Don't libel your competition.

Don't deceive your reader about your own product or service.

Problems for Classwork and Homework

P22.1 Analyze a Letter

Obtain a sales letter from your own or a friend's mail. If that proves impossible, your instructor may have left one or more samples on reserve in your library for use in this assignment. Analyze the letter in terms of the advice given in this chapter. How does the letter conform to and deviate from that advice? Turn in a copy of the letter along with your analysis.

P22.2 Club Letter

Write a sales letter to increase membership in your new college club. Think of the club as a "product" you are trying to sell. Invent the name and type of club. Determine who the audience for such a letter should be, and address the letter to that audience (for example, *Dear Science Major:*).

P22.3 Brochure

Do problem 22.2 but create a brochure instead of a traditional letter. Fold a piece of $8^1/_2 \times 7$ inch paper in half, lengthwise. This will result in four panels. On the front cover, put the organization's name and other important information, such as its location and phone number. Use the interior panels for promotion and information. Make panels attractive by employing a lot of white space, symmetrical and asymmetrical text blocks, and illustrations (examine some models from among the many brochures found in college offices). The back outside panel should serve as an envelope front. Put a return address in the upper left corner and leave the middle empty for a mass-mailing address sticker.

P22.4 Product Letter

Write a sales letter for one of the new products in the list below. Address it to past customers of your company's line of products (your mailing list is based on past orders). Invent details.

a. A do-it-yourself professional hair curler from the Home Hair Care Company
b. A set of knives from Total Kitchen
c. A fireplace screen from American Log Fires
d. A tree, bush, grass, or flowering plant for landscaping from Greg's Garden
e. An automobile seat cover from Wheels Ahead
f. A flea collar from Pet Please
g. An exotic beer from Suds City
h. A walking shoe from What's Afoot
i. A child-care video from Marriage, Inc.
j. A piece of computer software from the SoftSell Co.
k. A poetry series from Literati Publishers
l. A high-powered bullet from His & Hers Ammo

P22.5 Invent Product

Invent your own product or service and write a sales letter promoting it.

23

Oral Presentations

The success of an oral presentation depends to a great extent on planning. Whether you are arguing a case before your department bosses or presenting information about your company to the public, your success hinges on how well prepared you are at the outset. Here is some advice for carrying out that planning.

23.1 Describe Your Purpose and Audience

Define in writing what you want to achieve with your presentation. In college you get credit for "showing what you know," and it may be enough to stand up in class and talk about your subject knowledgeably, but in the business world you get credit for getting work done. Keep your practical purposes in mind while preparing your content.

Review section 5.1 in chapter 5, which lists characteristics of your audience you need to know, including their level of knowledge of the subject and their initial attitude toward your views. Use the information in section 5.1 to conduct a formal audience analysis before you start a presentation outline.

23.2 Do a Room Analysis

Analyze your speaking environment. Determine the size of the room, its acoustic quality, the lighting system, the location of electrical outlets, the kind of podium or table you will be speaking from and whether it can be placed conveniently for using a slide or overhead projector, whether or not a projection screen is behind the speaking platform, whether or not a microphone will be in place, whether or not photocopying will be available at the site, and anything else you can think of related to the mechanics of your performance.

You may have to adjust your approach to the presentation according to features of the environment. For example, if the room is large, people sitting in the back may have trouble seeing details in some of your visuals. Provide photocopies of those visuals so that your audience can consult the photocopy for details.

23.3 Create Two Outlines of Your Presentation

Two outlines will prove useful to your presentation. First, develop the content of your presentation by creating a detailed outline of all the information you wish to include. From that detailed outline create a second, simpler outline for use during your presentation. Limit it to major and second-level section headings. Include more detail only for those sections where you may forget what you want to say or where you will need facts and figures that won't appear in a visual. During your talk, you should only consult your presentation outline in discreet glances. Don't crowd it with so much writing that you can't find your main points. If you have to silently read your notes in order to find the next point, your presentation will momentarily stall.

Organize your talk around visuals. If you use overhead projections, make sure each new projection illustrates a new, important point, or another set of data supporting a point. As you present a new visual, pause to allow your audience to study it.

As a last step, review your presentation. Does its content match its purpose and audience? Will it do the job?

23.4 Rehearse

Practice your whole presentation. If you are using slides or overheads, and you don't have a projection system, pretend that you have one and go through all the motions necessary for the actual talk, including the changing of visuals. You don't want your movements to interrupt your speaking in the middle of an important point. Rehearsal allows you to coordinate movement and speech.

Practice talking slightly louder and a little bit slower than you normally do, especially if you normally speak rapidly. Modulate your voice so that its pitch varies. Monotonous speech is hard to understand and boring. Eliminate distracting hand movements and unnecessary body movements. Figure out where your hands will be most of the time. Find places to appropriately pause and gesture to emphasize a point. Learn to stand fairly still until you are ready to point to your visual or set up a new one. Look from the visual to the audience, not down at the floor or up at the ceiling.

23.5 Defeat Nervousness

Most people feel slightly nervous before making a presentation. Preparation reduces the anxiety. A good tip is to know exactly what you are going to say and do, word for word and gesture for gesture, in the first minute or so. After that point, nervousness usually disappears and rarely reappears if you are well prepared and know where you're headed every moment.

One good way to get started and eliminate nervousness is to build an audience participation component into the opening of your talk. Get the audience doing something, such as checking to see if their socks match, thinking up two reasons why they would do such-and-such, or interviewing each other on some question pertinent to your theme. Call on people to report. That kind of interactive activity loosens everyone up, including you, the speaker.

If you are prepared for bad moments, they won't throw you. Have a couple of joke lines ready for when the equipment fails, or you drop your pointer, or you lose your place in your speech, or you flub a line. Anticipate antagonistic questions at the end. If one comes along have a polite, short answer. In case someone really starts to get nasty, have a joke line ready to deflate the tension and get the rest of the audience on your side. But make the joke at your expense. Don't be discourteous.

Problems for Classwork and Homework

P23.1 Attend Presentation

Attend a speech on campus. Take notes on how closely the speaker follows the advice in this chapter. Include any other interesting observations. Write a memo report to your instructor based on your notes.

P23.2 Prepare a Presentation

Prepare an oral presentation for one of the scenarios below. Write a memo report to your instructor in which you discuss the purpose, the audience, and the room, and the technology you intend to use to create visuals. Provide a detailed outline with brief descriptions of the visuals. Provide a shorter presentation outline. Write out exactly what you intend to do during the first few minutes. List your joke lines. List antagonistic questions you anticipate and your responses.

a. You work in the purchasing department (or some other department) of a university (or a small company). You need to persuade the department and your bosses to purchase a new computer system (or file cabinet system, or telephone/fax/answering-machine system) for the desks in your offices.
b. You work for a company that sells magazines and books to retired people. You are scheduled at the local community center to make a presentation to seniors on your company's products. You'll be offering special discounts on purchases made after the presentation.

c. You have been invited to give a talk to the Youth Club on The Joys of Nature Walks (or league softball, or art appreciation, or any other hobby you are familiar with). Your purpose is to recruit new participants.
d. Create your own situation, topic, audience, and purpose.

P23.3 Give a Presentation

Prepare and deliver to your class one of the presentations in P23.2.

P23.4 Evaluate a Classmate

Evaluate a classmate's presentation. Demonstrate your understanding of the points made in this chapter by reviewing the presentation in terms of those points. Submit your report in a memo to your instructor.

24

Traditional Resumes

A **resume** (reh′-zu-may) is a one- or two-page summary of your qualifications for employment. You submit your resume when you apply for a job or a job interview. If you are completely unfamiliar with resumes, examine the model in Box 24.1.

Traditional resumes are printed on paper rather than posted electronically (the latter are discussed in chapter 26). Traditional resumes follow standard formats so that resume readers can easily interpret them and quickly find the information they require. Harried resume readers, overwhelmed with applications, look for reasons to reject a resume: a dirt spot on the paper, a sloppy layout, a misspelled word, a nonstandard approach that isn't immediately comprehensible. Your resume should have a clean, easy-to-read appearance, or it may be chucked into the rejection pile unread.

24.1 Targeting Your Resume

Whenever you apply for a specific job, put together a version of your resume that targets obvious characteristics of the job. The resume should specifically address qualifications mentioned in the job advertisement. Highlight the most relevant aspects of your education and experience. For example, in one version of your resume you might not include the fact that you took two years of Spanish in college, but you would highlight it in a resume targeted for a summer job as a playground coordinator in a neighborhood with a large Spanish-speaking population.

Before writing a targeted resume, analyze the advertisement. Consider this sample ad:

> WANTED: An independent go-getter willing to put in long hours to make big returns as a supervisor of a popular retail outlet. Sales experience and basic knowledge of bookkeeping preferred.

To analyze this advertisement, look for key words that reveal what the ad writer is looking for. In this case, some of the key words are: *independent* (can you work alone without close supervision? are you the kind of person

Box 24.1

Reverse Chronological Resume

Larry Fernandez

980 Front Street
Albright, NY 38756
(453) 675-9076

OBJECTIVE: Management position working with animals.

SUMMARY: Experienced pet store worker. Junior-year environmental science major with management minor. Know how to keep books and records and how to manage workers.

Work Experience

1994–Present: Animal lab assistant for Biology Department, SUNY Albright

1991–93 Butchy's Restaurant, 453 McClellen St., Schenectady, NY 34297

- Waiter for evening shift

1988–91 Grindstone Pet Mart, 11 Hoover Way, Aldo, NY 34298

- Performed all maintenance jobs required for a wide range of animals, including birds, cats, dogs, rabbits, snakes, lizards, and frogs.
- Sold animals and pet care products.

Education

Biology major, State University of New York, Albright. Seventy-six credits toward degree in Environmental Science track. Twelve credits in business.

Courses taken include:

—General Zoology
—Comparative Vertebrate Anatomy
—Ethology
—Business Administration
—Accounting I & II
—Marketing

Hobby

Enter my trained Newfoundland in water trials.

who takes the initiative to solve problems?); *go-getter* (are you ambitious, someone who wants to achieve the best sales record in the company?); *supervisor* (do you have experience managing people?); *bookkeeping preferred* (if you don't know bookkeeping, will you have learned the basics on your own by the time you show up for the interview?).

24.2 Types of Resumes

Despite the many combinations and variations possible, there are basically only two types of resumes. The most common, and still the most popular among professionals in large personnel departments, is the **reverse chronological** resume. The reverse chronological resume presents your educational background, starting with your latest degree or enrollment, followed by your work experience, beginning with your most recent job. After that you may include personal information and special skills.

The other main type is the **functional** resume, which features statements of your abilities. Education and work experience are mentioned briefly at the end to verify your claims.

Boxes 24.1 and 24.2 contrast the reverse chronological and functional styles. Many resume writers successfully combine these approaches into a "mixed style," which begins with skills and presents an extensive employment and educational history in reverse chronological order.

24.3 General Principles of Form and Appearance

Print your resume with a laser printer on high-quality white paper. Use the standard formats mentioned above or a combination of reverse chronological and functional.

Unless you have a long work history and you are applying for a senior position, stick to one or two pages. Number additional pages after the first at the top or bottom. Include your name on each page after the first, in case the pages get separated. Do not staple pages together. Be sure that your text is free of typographical or spelling errors.

24.4 General Principles of Content and Style

Your resume should tell the reader (1) what you can do for the target organization, (2) what personal characteristics of yours will help the target organization, and (3) what education and experience (work, volunteer, membership, or any other) backs up your claims. Prefer verb phrases to

Box 24.2

Functional Resume

980 Front Street, Albright, NY 38756 (453) 675-9076

Larry Fernandez

Goal: Pet Store Manager

Animal Expertise

Three years experience in pet store:

- Maintained a variety of animals including birds, cats, dogs, rabbits, snakes, lizards, and frogs
- Sold animals and pet care products
- As biology major (junior-year status) have taken courses in zoology, comparative vertebrate anatomy, and ethology
- Trained my Newfoundland for water trials.

Management Expertise

As management minor in college, took courses in:

- business management
- accounting (to advanced level)
- marketing

Employment

1994–Present:	Animal lab assistant for Biology Department, SUNY Albright
1991–93	Butchy's Restaurant, 453 McClellen St., Schenectady, NY 34297 —Waiter for evening shift
1988–91	Grindstone Pet Mart, 11 Hoover Way, Aldo, NY 34298

Education

Biology major, State University of New York, Albright. Seventy-six credits toward degree in Environmental Science track. Twelve credits in business.

full sentences: "sold more than 300 encyclopedias"; "managed 12 people." Use parallel structure (see chapter 8) and the same indentations for comparable items.

Don't lie about your background. Don't exaggerate your abilities or accomplishments. Instead, focus on your strong qualities. Any shortcomings that you must admit in order to remain honest, you can mention in the cover letter that accompanies your resume. The resume is not a place to *explain* things.

24.5 Standard Resume Sections

Some of the following sections appear in all resumes; others (as indicated) are optional. The sections are presented in the order in which they most commonly appear from top to bottom on the resume.

24.5a The Heading

All headings should contain your name in a prominent position, your "permanent" address (where you know mail can reach you), and your phone number. If you have a fax number or an e-mail address, put that in. Box 24.3 shows some layouts for headings.

24.5b Objective (Optional)

Many resumes include an OBJECTIVE line after the heading. This line tells the resume reader what kind of a job you are looking for. In a resume targeted for a specific advertisement, you can tailor this line to the job. For example, for a job managing women's shoe sales in a department store:

> OBJECTIVE: Sales manager, using my education in business and my experience in retail sales.

This statement should always be fairly specific. Don't say that you want an "entry-level position in a small business." On the other hand, if you put a specific objective on a resume, you may eliminate yourself from job opportunities at the target company other than the one specifically advertised. If you are open to a broad range of occupations, consider leaving this element out of your resume.

24.5c Summary of Qualifications (Optional)

The summary of qualifications is a short paragraph or short list naming your strongest assets. Place it just below the heading. The purpose of

Box 24.3

Layouts for the Resume Heading

Kent Gordon
132 Oak Street
Mobile, AL 37648
(978) 555-0978

Kent Gordon
132 Oak Street
Mobile, AL 37648
(978) 555-0978

Kent Gordon
133 Oak Street, Mobile, AL 37648 PH (978) 879-0978 E-mail: kgordon@aol.com

Kent Gordon
133 Oak Street
Mobile, AL 37648
(978) 879-0978
E-mail: kgordon@aol.com

Kent Gordon

Before 5-10-98
133 Oak Street
Mobile, AL 37648
(978) 555-0978

After 5-10-98
342 Peach Street
Coalsville, PA 15417
(412) 555-0978

the summary is to interest the reader in the rest of your resume. Here's an example:

> MAJOR QUALIFICATIONS
> B.S. Degree in biology. Experienced in designing and carrying out wildlife studies and presenting results at conferences. Experienced in grant writing.

By reading the summary, the resume reader can tell at a glance if you are the kind of person the organization is looking for. If so, the resume reader will continue reading with special interest.

24.5d Education

State first your major or degree earned followed by the name of the school. Begin with the school you are now attending or last attended. Follow with the second most recent, and so on. Do not list high schools, but do list community colleges and technical schools. Include your grade point average if you are proud of it.

Mention college-related certifications, memberships, honors, and activities either here, under EDUCATION, or in separate sections. In a resume targeted for a specific job advertisement, you may wish to list courses you took that relate to the job. Or you may wish to simply write, "Computer science: 15 credits."

24.5e Experience

Most resume readers prefer candidates with work experience, even if it is low-level summer work or part-time employment. Include the address (city and state) of the employer and the dates of employment. Also include a statement of your duties, responsibilities, and acquired skills:

> Opened and closed the shop; dealt with customers; handled orders from regular vendors; reconciled the register at closing.

"Experience" can mean more than the jobs you've held. College students and recent college graduates may not have much work experience. If that is the case with you, include other activities that gave you potentially useful experience:

> —On Colorado River raft trip learned the importance of teamwork under stressful conditions; learned organizational skills as coordinator of Special Olympics.

—As a volunteer library worker, learned computer skills, people skills, and organizational skills.

24.5f Awards, Honors, Memberships (Optional)

You can dip back into your high school years to bring out something truly impressive, such as "Eagle Scout" or "Traveled to France with school quartet." Here are some examples from college-student resumes:

PTA scholarship; Dean's List three years; Coach's Award: track and field; Alpha Kappa Lambda fraternal organization, elected treasurer two years; elected to student government; elected to dorm council; German Club; Candy Striper; member, NCTE; won writing award for best freshman essay.

24.5g Special Skills And Certifications (Optional)

Include skills that might be useful to the kind of work environment you are trying to enter, but also those that have a social function, such as "scratch golfer." Here are some examples from college-student resumes:

Fluent in Spanish, can get along in French; familiar with Mac and DOS hardware and software; know Windows and word processing, can use computer databases and spreadsheets; certified lifeguard (or scuba diver or First Aid and CPR); tennis instructor; editor of high school newspaper.

24.5h Personal Interests, Hobbies, Activities (Optional)

A list of your personal interests helps demonstrate your ability to get along with others and the fact that you are an energetic and active person. Sometimes you get lucky and these interests are shared by the person doing the hiring. Here are typical examples from college-student resumes:

Tennis, golf, sailing, sports fan, Little League coach, camping, travel to foreign countries, bridge, gardening club, coin collecting.

You can also suggest an intellectual or creative side to your character:

Reading poetry; painting in watercolors; playing guitar; attending symphonies; reading American history and visiting historical places.

24.5i Your Own Subheadings (Optional)

So far, this section has considered either standard categories found in all resumes or common optional categories. Don't hesitate to invent your own categories and appropriate subheadings. If you have had a successful career in the military, for instance, you might want to make Military Experience a subheading. If you have done a lot of charitable work, you may want to create a special category for that: Charitable Work. Use your imagination to create a resume that fits you and highlights your experience and accomplishments.

24.5j Multimedia Addendum (Optional)

In some professions, such as education or art, it may make sense to develop an addendum to your resume on a computer disk that might display a video of you teaching a class or a gallery of your art work. Such a disk should accompany your written resume, not substitute for it.

24.6 References

Ideally, you should cultivate good relations with professors before finishing college so that they will be willing to write you good recommendations. Ask people from whom you would like references if they would be willing to speak on your behalf to prospective employers who call them, and if they would be willing to write a recommendation for you. When you have established a list of people willing to serve as your references, provide each of them with an informal outline of the points you wish them to make. For example:

- — Attended my Cost Accounting I and Business Ethics courses; earned A's in both courses.
- — Wrote a well-researched A paper for Business Ethics on how Exxon should have handled the Valdez oil spill.
- — Hard worker; dependable.
- — Dresses neatly; maintains friendly, respectful manner.

A professor might teach a hundred or more students every year. Such a list of points serves as a reminder of who you are and what you accomplished in the professor's course.

If the job advertisement that you are responding to specifically asks for references, list the names, addresses, and phone numbers on a separate sheet of paper and add it to the resume.

Problems for Classwork and Homework

P24.1 List Awards, Honors, Accomplishments

Create a list of possible awards, honors, memberships, special skills, important interests, and unusual experiences that you might be able to fit into your resume. Share these with your group or the class and note entries on other students' lists that you might have overlooked among your own accomplishments. If possible, expand your list before turning it in.

P24.2 Analyze Qualifications

Find a job or internship advertisement for which you might qualify in a newspaper or some other publication. Select an advertisement that lists qualifications for applicants; the more detailed, the better. Write a two-column analysis of the match between your qualifications and those listed in the advertisement. Write a memo to your instructor discussing how well they match. Note any qualifications that you don't match perfectly but might cover with similar experience or an ability to learn.

P24.3 Reverse Chronological Resume

Photocopy an advertisement. Write a reverse chronological resume that fits your qualifications to those named in the advertisement. Include a "Summary" statement at the top, below your heading. Turn in the photocopied ad along with your resume.

P24.4 Functional Resume

Follow the steps in P24.3 but create a functional resume.

P24.5 Dream Resume

Write a dream resume, the resume you would like to be able to write when you graduate from college. Be realistic—dream does not mean fantasy. Think of this resume as a plan or set of goals for the next few years.

Box 24.4

Resume — Strong Education, Weak Experience

Michelle Martin

214 Elm Street, Tuscan, AZ 43674
(645) 873-9080/martin@brim.com

Education

Bachelor of Arts in Travel and Tourism/Graduation in May 1997
Summit State College, Marklesburg, AZ

—Dual minors in French and German
—President of Travel Club
—Took courses in computer database management and accounting
—Spent two summers in Europe, traveling extensively
—Took 12 credits in European history

College Activities

—In charge of the Travel and Tourism College Career Fair in senior year
—Student government representative, two years
—Residence Hall Council, one year
—Treasurer of Phi Alpha Psi service sorority, three years
—Women's intercollegiate tennis team, three years

Awards and Honors

—Nominated for Best Travel and Tourism Major in junior year
—Recipient of Eloise Makin Scholarship for Women ($500)
—Earned first prize in high school writing contest

Experience

1994–1996—Lonesome Steer Steak House, 11 Market Street, Tuscan
- Waitress and cashier

1991–1995—Volunteer work: Tuscan Recreation Committee
- Organized summer activities for 6– to 10–year-olds
- Helped arrange cultural events for the city

Box 24.5

Two-page Resume — Strong Experience

Maria Stroppolo

1536 Ginger Street
Newton, PA 17865

(413) 765-9087
stroppolo@aol.com

MANAGER

Assistant manager for Clarktown, Pennsylvania, Simmons Oil gas station (1996–present):

- Did paperwork for gasoline and store product sales
- Constructed time-saving process for the daily checkout
- Trained new employees
- Arranged work shifts for new employees

Manager of Bolton's Fish Market, Clarktown, Pennsylvania (1992–96):

- Supervised 8 employees
- Ordered all products
- Did the bookkeeping
- Opened a lunch bar on the premises, which became very profitable

Employee of Newton, Pennsylvania, Park Service (1987–90, summers):

- Supervised five summer employees
- Oversaw maintenance of park facilities, including lawn and garden landscaping and the upkeep of buildings

COMPUTER USER

- Completed 15 credits of computer science
- Tutored CARE project students in DOS and Mac word processing
- Used my own computer and modem at home to do research on the Internet for college papers.

Box 24.5 *continued*

Two-page Resume — Strong Experience

Maria Stroppolo
Page 2

PROFESSIONAL WRITER

Volunteer for the Clarktown *Senior Times* magazine (1990–present):

- Write responses to inquiries and complaints from subscribers
- Research and write articles at the request of the editor

STUDENT

1982–84 B.A. Management, Pumpkinville College, 3.2 QPA
1981–82 24 credits, Clarkville Junior College, 3.4 QPA

ATHLETE

—Tenth year in Clarkville Women's Softball League
—Avid golfer

25

Job-Search Letters

A job search involves not only resume writing but also letter writing. Never mail a resume without including a cover letter, which introduces you, states that you are applying for a job, and develops your qualifications. Even if you are responding to a job advertisement that merely says, "Send resume to . . .", you should accompany your resume with a cover letter.

If you haven't heard from your prospective employer within a week, you can write a follow-up letter that reminds him or her of your interest in the advertised job or the organization. If you are offered a job, you must write a letter of acceptance or rejection.

25.1 Cover Letters

Cover letters discuss your qualifications but do not supply supporting information. The factual support for your claims will be found in your enclosed resume, which you should refer to early in your cover letter: "As my resume shows, I have three years experience. . . ." You also remind the reader that your resume is enclosed by putting the word *Enclosure* at the bottom left of your cover letter, below the closing (see chapter 2 on letter format).

The cover letter is an opportunity to sell yourself unabashedly. Tell the reader what you have done for other organizations. Tell the reader what you can do for the target organization. Describe your character: hard working, reliable, enthusiastic, competent, or whatever seems appropriate and accurately reflects your nature.

25.2 Unsolicited vs. Solicited Cover Letters

Cover letters can be divided into two groups: unsolicited and solicited (or ad response). An **unsolicited** letter goes out to an employer that you believe may be hiring or about to hire people with your qualifications. You might also send such letters to employment agencies.

The best way to find a job is to use your personal contacts. Therefore, the best target for a successful unsolicited letter is a person you know, or a person whom a friend, relative, or acquaintance knows. In the latter case, you should mention the person who referred you and indicate your relationship to that person:

> I play tennis with Bob Pearson, who works in your sales department, and Bob suggested that I contact you about a possible opening in your accounting office.

By making such a suggestion, Bob Pearson, a person within the organization, is making an implied recommendation.

When you aren't aware of any specific job opportunity or job requirements, the unsolicited cover letter must be rather general in covering your abilities (see Box 25.1 for an example). In contrast, cover letters in response to job advertisements provide you an opportunity to address specific job requirements mentioned in the advertisement. Take note of every qualification listed in the ad; don't ignore any of them. You must directly demonstrate how you meet every qualification, or that you have knowledge, ability, or experience in the area or in a related area, or that in some other way you can handle the requirement:

> Your advertisement specifically mentions tree planting. My experience with landscaping is limited to lawns and bushes, but I am a quick learner and I have no doubt that I can transfer my skill in planting bushes to planting trees.

You can also mention qualifications that logically suit you for the job, even if they are not mentioned in the advertisement.

25.3 Cover Letter: Possibilities for the Beginning

Start by introducing yourself ("I am a recent college graduate with a major in chemistry looking for a job in. . . ."). If responding to an advertisement, say so ("I am interested in the opening you advertised in the *Miami Herald* for 'an experienced school counselor.'") Mention any contacts you have with the organization ("I am a friend of Louise Shelton, a secretary in your main office. . . ."). Identify yourself in terms of your general qualifications ("As my resume indicates, I am an experienced school counselor. . . .").

25.4 Cover Letter: Possibilities for the Middle

Use the middle portion of your cover letter to sell yourself by showing how your qualifications match those mentioned in the advertisement.

Box 25.1

Unsolicited Cover Letter

145 Simpson Drive
Peritown, PA 15760
March 30, 19__

Mr. James Carib
Director of Parks, County of Washington
312 Peach Avenue
Washington, PA 15301

Dear Mr. Carib:

As a recent college graduate with a B.A. in Parks and Recreational Management, I am looking for a position in park management. As my resume indicates, I have an excellent academic background and useful experience in this field. If your department has an opening, my ability to get along with all sorts of people and to get jobs done well and on time, as well as my creativity in solving problems and developing new programs, make me an excellent candidate.

As a Parks and Recreation Management student, I accomplished the following:

- Earned a 3.4 overall QPA, 3.9 in my major.
- Completed courses in accounting and computer database management in addition to the park management requirements. These extra courses gave me the ability to maintain a complex budget.
- Served as treasurer in the Parks and Recreation Club and established a computer accounting system for the club using Lotus 1-2-3's integrated database and spreadsheet. The club now gets an accurate printed update of its accounts at each monthly meeting.

As a summer worker for Peritown Central Park, I acquired a variety of experience:

- Supervised six high school workers.
- Managed the landscaping one year; managed women's daytime sports leagues one year.
- Developed a new way to schedule games to avoid conflicts within a shorter season.

With my qualifications, I am confident that I can take on any available job in parks management. I would welcome an opportunity to discuss any openings at your facility in an interview. Please call me at (412) 555-9087 or e-mail me at rstevens@link.com.

Thank you for considering my application.

Sincerely,

Richard Stevens

Enclosure

You can use a bulleted list, as in a resume, or you can just describe yourself in normal paragraphs. Refer to your education and experience. If possible, use phrases from the advertisement:

> Your advertisement calls for a recreation director with "experience teaching outdoor sports to young children." I worked for three summers in a city park program in Atlanta coaching baseball for under-ten-year-olds. During that time I developed a good sense of how to deal with children this young as they learn outdoor sports. I understand the various personalities and needs of these children, and I am good at inspiring them all to participate to the maximum of their abilities.

25.5 Cover Letter: Possibilities for the End

Conclude your cover letter by stating what you want your reader to do—most likely set up an interview. Make it easy by including your phone number and when you can be reached. End with a "thank you" of some sort. Here is a typical conclusion:

> If my qualifications interest you, I would like to discuss this position further in an interview at your location. I can be reached at (412) 555-8976 after 3:00 p.m., or you can leave a message on my answering machine. I can take time off work for an interview any time in the next several weeks.
>
> Thank you for considering me for this position.

Box 25.2 provides an example of a solicited, ad-response cover letter.

25.6 Follow-Up Letters

A week after a job interview, especially one that you think was successful, send the interviewer a follow-up letter. A follow-up letter reminds the interviewer of your qualifications and emphasizes your interest in working for the organization. Arrange your letter in three parts:

THE BEGINNING: Thank the interviewer for taking the time to interview you and provide you with information about the organization. Mention your admiration for the organization.

THE MIDDLE: Remind the interviewer of your qualifications and how they fit what you learned about the organization from the

Box 25.2

Solicited (Ad Response) Cover Letter

In response to this ad: **ACCOUNTANT** Duff County CPA firm seeks experienced accountant. Must have payroll tax experience and general ledger skills. Computer skills a plus. Apply to Box 76389, c/o the *Duff Daily News,* 967 Main Street, Princeton, OR 48390

March 30, 1996

500 Graham Avenue
Partridgeville, OR 48390

Box 76389
c/o *Duff Daily News*
967 Main Street
Princeton, OR 48390

Re: Accounting position

I am applying for the accounting position advertised in the March 28th edition of the *Duff Daily News*. I have an accounting degree from Oregon State University, and I worked for three years as a student assistant to the financial manager for the Duff County Senior Citizens Center. I am now working there full time as an accountant.

As my enclosed resume shows, I have carried out a range of duties at the Senior Center, including payroll and general ledger.

Your advertisement indicated a desire for computer skills. I have a thorough knowledge of Lotus 1-2-3. At the Senior Center I am in charge of all database management. I installed and operate a computerized accounting system (MYOB) and a computerized fundraising program (Kenrick).

If my qualifications interest you, I am available for an interview on Wednesday or Friday afternoons. I can take short phone calls at work: (745) 793-9042. I have an answering machine on my home phone: (745) 733-8796. I can also be reached any time via e-mail: keye@techno.com.

My salary requirements are in the $35K to $45K range, depending on work load and responsibilities. Thank you for your consideration.

Very truly yours,

Louise Keye

Encl.

interview. Mention some detail about the organization that impressed you.

THE END: Reassert your interest in working for the organization. Finish with a friendly, optimistic closure. Box 25.3 provides an example of a follow up letter.

25.7 Acceptance and Rejection Letters

When you have decided whether to accept or reject a job offer, immediately write back to the organization informing them of your decision. An acceptance letter states at the outset that you are pleased to take the job. Make clear what you are agreeing to by restating any condition of employment mentioned in the letter or the conversation in which you were offered the job, such as salary, rank, or date the employment begins. End with a friendly closing statement: "I look forward to joining the team at West Mooring Products."

If you don't want the job, immediately write a rejection letter to inform the organization that they need to find someone else. As a practical matter, never burn bridges to possible employers by arrogantly ignoring their offer.

Begin your rejection letter by stating that although you admire the organization you cannot accept their job offer. Explain why. Perhaps you have already accepted an offer elsewhere, or the salary offered isn't high enough and you intend to keep looking for a job that pays more. Be honest. End with a friendly closing statement, possibly wishing the organization good luck in its job search.

Boxes 25.4 and 25.5 provide examples of acceptance and rejection letters.

Problems for Classwork and Homework

P25.1 Unsolicited Cover Letter

Write an unsolicited cover letter to a local company. Assume that you heard about a job due to open up at this company for which you feel qualified. The inside information came from your neighbor Howard Riley, who works as a technical writer for the company.

P25.2 Analyze Job Ads

Put together a collection of recent advertisements for job openings or internships in your specialty. Find one from a newspaper, one from a trade magazine, and one from your school's placement office. Look in particular for entry-level positions that you could logically apply for now or upon graduation from college. Pick advertisements that name specific job

Box 25.3

Follow-Up Letter

440 Market Street
Apt. 7B
Coaltown, PA 15411
June 18, 19__

Ms. Jackie Bartlett
Production Supervisor
Parkway Foods
4000 Dunning Avenue
Bolton, PA 14743

Dear Ms. Bartlett:

I enjoyed my interview with you and Mr. Schrader at Parkway Foods last Monday, and I want to thank you for taking the time to show me around the facilities. I was impressed by the physical plant and the energetic, professional work force. Parkway strikes me as the kind of place where my diligent work style can get full play.

I especially liked the mingling of line workers with their managers at lunch and the prework meetings at which problems are discussed. Supervisors at Parkway are indeed able to benefit from these friendly interchanges.

If you have any questions about my resume, please call me at (565) 873-5555, or e-mail me at jminx@aol.com.

Sincerely,

James Minx

Box 25.4

Acceptance Letter

Dear Ms. Bartlett:

I am pleased to accept your job offer for the position of assistant sales manager at Parkway Foods. As your letter states, this job pays $32,500, plus the benefits described in the booklet you gave me at my interview.

You asked if I can begin by August 10. I will have no problem starting on that date. Tomorrow I will give my two-weeks' notice to my present employer, and that will leave me almost a week to get settled in the Bolton area. In fact, I hope to come in a day or two early to handle the paperwork with the personnel department and perhaps meet a few more of my coworkers.

I am looking forward to working for Parkway Foods.

Sincerely,

Box 25.5

Rejection Letter

Dear Ms. Bartlett:

I just received your letter offering me the position of assistant sales manger at Parkway Foods. I must decline the offer because I have already accepted a job at another food distributor.

I am flattered to have received the offer. Parkway struck me as an excellent employer, and I enjoyed the interview with you and Mr. Schrader. I wish you luck in filling the assistant sales manager position.

Sincerely,

requirements and analyze those requirements in relation to your qualifications. Do this by making a two-column list. On the left side, list each job requirement. On the right side, indicate how your abilities and experience meet that requirement. Type up the dual column lists and turn them in along with a copy of the advertisements.

P25.3 Ad Response Cover Letter

Create an appropriate cover letter in response to an actual advertisement for a job opening or internship in your specialty. Select an advertisement that names specific job requirements. Turn in a copy of the advertisement along with the cover letter.

P25.4 Tire Company

You interviewed well at Kobler, Inc., a large tire manufacturer in your hometown. You were impressed by the office staff that you would be supervising, as well as by the friendliness and qualifications of the technical professionals to whom you were introduced. Write a follow-up letter to Ms. Benmartin, who interviewed you. Invent details.

P25.5 Business Instructor

You just interviewed for a work-study job as assistant to your business writing instructor, who is creating a course packet for the department's "Business Writing II" course. Now you realize that you forgot to make an important point about your qualifications (invent this point). Write a follow-up letter to your business writing instructor.

26 Electronic Job Search

Although personal contacts remain the best way to get a job, computers available at colleges and universities can also enhance your job search. The computer indexes at most post-secondary school libraries can put you in touch with relevant periodicals and books. The Internet's World Wide Web (WWW) provides sites for learning about job-search techniques, for gaining information about companies and professions, for finding job advertisements, for connecting with job-search companies, and for posting or submitting your resume and cover letter.

26.1 Using Electronic Indexes to Find Print Resources

Your school library probably has electronic indexes for journals, trade magazines, books, and other print resources. By entering key words such as "job search," you can search those indexes for articles in periodicals such as the *National Business Employment Weekly* and *Job Choices*. You can also locate useful books such as the following:

Bolles, R. N. (1997). *Job-Hunting on the Internet.* Berkeley: Ten Speed Press.

Gonyea, J. C. (1995). *The on-line job search companion: A complete guide to hundreds of career planning and job hunting resources available via your computer.* New York: McGraw-Hill.

Kennedy, J. L. (1994). *Electronic job search revolution: Win with the new technology that's reshaping today's job market.* New York: J. Wiley.

Munschauer, J. L., (1982). *Jobs for English majors and other smart people.* Princeton, NJ: Peterson's Guides, Inc.

Parker, Y. (1989). *The damn good resume guide.* Berkeley: Ten Speed Press.

Note that the Munschauer entry above addresses a particular major, English. Your major also can serve as a key word in your library and Internet searches. See Box 26.1 for Internet sites related to academic majors.

26.2 Using Your Phone to Access Company Joblines

Joblines are recorded phone messages that companies leave for job seekers. If you call an organization's jobline, you will hear up-to-date information on job openings within that organization, including the necessary qualifications and who you should write to at what address.

A useful list of jobline phone numbers appears in Marcia Williams and Sue Cubbage's book *The 1995 National Job Hotline Directory.* The authors list organizations by state and by profession. The 1995 edition of their book lists about thirty-five hundred phone numbers. You can also find jobline numbers for companies by searching the World Wide Web on the Internet.

26.3 Finding Job Resources on the World Wide Web

To find World Wide Web resources you must use a search engine, a program that looks through databases posted on the Internet. When you arrive at a search engine site, use the menu provided to find the kind of resource you are looking for (job ads, resume-writing techniques, company information, and so forth) or search by key words. Each search engine uses its own search methods and its own list of databases, so try more than one. Here are the locations of some of the most popular search engines:

Yahoo	http://www.yahoo.com
Galaxy	http://galaxy.tradewave.com
Altavista	http://www.altavista.digital.com
HotBot	http://www.hotbot.com
WebCrawler	http://webcrawler.com
Lycos	http://www.lycos.com

Industry and other job-related information is listed at on-line databases such as these:

The Clearinghouse	http://www.clearinghouse.net
Hoover's On-line	http://www.hoovers.com
ComFind	http://www.comfind.com

You can read the classified section of major newspapers at sites such as these:

New York Times	http://www.nytimes.com
Washington Post	http://www.washingtonpost.com

Box 26.1

Web Sites Listing Job Advertisements

General Job Listings

America's Job Bank http://www.ajb.dni.us/
Links with public employment services, employers' job sites, and private placement agencies' site of 706 listings.
NationJob Online Jobs Database http://www.nationjob.com/
Lists various jobs by category in "Specialty Pages."
The Monster Board http://www.monster.com/
Includes a section for entry-level jobs.
Yahoo Classified http://classifieds.yahoo.com/
Helpwanted.com http://www.helpwanted.com/
JobWeb http://www.jobweb.org/
Job Bank USA http://www.jobbankusa.com/
On Line Career Center http://www.occ.com/occ/Jobseeker.html
A well-organized site with interesting articles on campus issues.
Career Mosaic http://www.careermosaic.com/cm/jobs.html
A unique site for college students, with writing clinic for resume writing, besides job listings.
4Work http://www.4work.com
Includes jobs for volunteers, internships, part-time work. Allows you to leave your e-mail address to be notified for job vacancies.
Careerpath http://www.careerpath.com
Lists the latest help-wanted ads from 41 newspapers.
Career Magazine http://www.careermag.com
Daily downloads and indexes all of the job postings from the major Internet jobs newsgroups.
Federal Jobs Digest http://www.jobsfed.com/
Daily updates on vacancies in federal government jobs.
Cool Works http://www.coolworks.com/
Information on jobs in ski resorts, Club Med, cruise ships, national parks.
Summer Jobs http://www.summerjobs.com/do/
Not limited to summer jobs.
Job Smart http://jobsmart.org/
A good site if you are looking for a job in California.
Career City http://www.careercity.com
Links to hundreds of other sites of interest to job seekers.
Job Hunt http://www.job-hunt.org

Job Listings for Special Interests

Working Solo http://www.workingsolo.com
A center for resources to help you start and grow a successful business as an independent entrepreneur.
Small Business Administration http://www.sbaonline.sba.gov/
A helpful site for the self-employed.
Women's Wire http://www.women.com/work/best/
Includes 100 best companies for working mothers.
Action without Borders, Inc. http://www.idealist.org/IS/job_search.html
A site for nonprofit organization job seekers.

Box 26.1 *continued*

Web Sites Listing Job Advertisements

Job Accommodations Network http://www.jan.wvu.edu/english/emptips.htm
"Employment tips" section provides "Employment Resource List" for job seekers with disabilities.
Resources for Minorities http://www.vjf.com/pub/docs/jobsearch.html

For the New Graduate

Entry Level Job Seeker Assistant http://members.aol.com/Dylander/jobhome.html
Jobtrak http://www.jobtrak.com
Designed for college students and alumni in conjunction with the career centers of various universities.
Student Center http://www.studentcenter.com
Good advice on many subjects.

Jobs By Major

Bio Online's Career Center http://bio.com/hr/
For biology majors.
100 Careers in Wall Street http://www.globalvillage.com/villager/WSC.html
For business majors.
Corporation for Public Broadcasting http://www.cpb.org/jobline/index.html
For communication/media majors.
Comrise Technology http://www.comrise.com/joblink.html
For computer science and technology majors.
Westech Virtual Job Fair http://www.vjf.com
For computer science and technology majors.
Jobs Jobs Jobs http://www.jobsjobsjobs.com/
For computer science and technology majors.
1-800 Network http://www.1800network.com
For computer science and technology majors.
E-Span http://www.espan.com/job/
For computer science and technology majors.
Education Jobs Marketplace http://www.edjobs.com/edjobs/
Engineering Jobs http://www.engineeringjobs.com/
Environmental Careers Organization http://www.eco.org/
Environmental science majors: internships and jobs.
MedSearch Healthcare Careers http://www.medsearch.com/
For health care majors, such as nursing, therapy, pharmaceutical.
Psychweb http://gasou.edu/psychweb/
For psychology majors. Visit the site page "Career Issues and Job Listings relating to Psychology"
http://gasou.edu/psychweb/resource/bytopic.htm#career.
Social Work and Social Services Jobs on Line http://128.252.132.4/jobs/
Social work majors.

Miami Herald	http://www.herald.com
Los Angeles Times	http://www.latimes.com

26.4 Handling Outdated Site Addresses

All the addresses in this book are at least one year old, and your attempts to access them may occasionally be frustrated by a message saying that the site cannot be found. This is because some sites just plain disappear (perhaps the person posting the information sold her computer and bought a loom). Often sites are rearranged as they are expanded, and addresses for particular pages may be revised and old addresses abandoned.

Sites most prone to difficulty are those that have a long page address, such as this one: **http://www.gasou.edu/psychweb/psych.htm**. In fact, this page no longer exists, and you'll get a "can't find" message when you try to go there. However, such a page may exist under another name, or the information the page once contained may reside at the same general site but inserted into other pages. When you fail to find a specific page, try shortening the address. First try reducing the address to one level beyond the classifying extension: com, org, edu, or net. For instance, reduce the psychology site mentioned above to **http://www.gasou.edu/psychweb**. If that doesn't work, reduce further to the general site: **http://www.gasou.edu**. When you arrive at the general site you will probably have to voyage through several menus to get to the information you are looking for, but the information may well be there, waiting to be found.

26.5 Finding a Job on the Internet

One way to find a job on the Internet is to access job listings and send out your resume and cover letter. Some job sites ask you to send your resume on-line, and some of those prefer that you use their own on-line resume form, in which you answer questions about yourself by filling in blanks. Box 26.1 provides a list of some of the best general-interest job-list sites, as well as a sampling of job-list sites categorized by special interest and by academic majors.

You can also post your resume at various sites in the hope that a company searching for someone with your qualifications and interests will come across it. Some job-posting sites charge a fee; others are free. Many sites listed in Box 26.1 allow you to post your resume, but Box 26.2 lists sites that specialize in this service.

Plan and proofread your on-line resume as carefully as you would a printed version. Don't assume that mistakes in an electronic text are any

Box 26.2

Sites for Posting Your Resume

Comrise Technology http://www.comrise.com/joblink.html
Technology oriented jobs for engineers, systems analysts, programmers, etc.

Career Magazine http://www.careermag.com

Jobtrak http://www.jobtrak.com

Harbornet Resume Listing
http://www.harbornet.com/biz/office/annex4htm
Listing by occupation. Will cost you $45/year.

Career Mosaic http://www.careermosaic.com/cm/cm39.html

Westech Virtual Job Fair http://www.vjf.com/pub/Rsubmit.html

E-span http://www.espan.com/

Box 26.3

Sites for Learning to Write Electronic Resumes

Advanced Resume Concepts
http://www.jtr.com/reslady/elec.htm

Electronic Resume Articles
http://canada.careermosaic.com/cm/crc35.html

Preparing the Ideal Scannable Resume
http://www.resumix.com/resume/resume_tips.html

Intel: How to Submit Your Resume
http://www.intel.com/intel/oppty/submit/index.htm

more acceptable than in a paper document. In fact, if your electronic resume interests the employer, it will probably be printed out and processed like a resume that arrived in an envelope.

26.6 Creating Resumes and Cover Letters in ASCII

Before you post your resume and cover letter on the Internet, or before you send them via e-mail to an employer, you must first convert these documents to ASCII (pure text). Every modern word-processing program has a process for doing that. This conversion means that underlining, italics, and other font manipulations will be lost. To format an effective ASCII resume, use a simple block-style design with uppercase headings and blank lines between sections (see Box 26.4). The same goes for cover letters. Use the simplest block style.

Even if the site does not ask for a cover letter, send one anyway, if possible. If the organization provides a postal address, send your resume and cover letter by mail as well. Mention in your cover letter that you also submitted your application documents to the organization's e-mail address.

26.7 Creating a Scannable Resume

Before you post, e-mail, or mail your resume to a potential employer, you must decide whether to send a conventional resume or a scannable resume. Any large employer, whether government agency or private corporation, is likely to review resumes first with scan-and-search software. This software converts the text of a submitted resume to ASCII, scans it into its database of resumes, and searches the resume for key words related to the required qualifications for the job. To compete with other applicants, you will have to compose your resume so that your information contains the key words that the employer will search for. The process is complicated by the fact that, although a human reader will recognize synonyms for designated key words, the scanning software may not.

The best way to eliminate key-word guessing games is to list key words in a summary section at the beginning of your resume, using nouns instead of verbs as your strong words. The traditional resume calls for strong verbs to demonstrate what you can do: *supervised* ten employees, *taught* Lotus 1-2-3, *improved* the purchasing process. But scan-and-search software programs look for nouns: *supervisor, instructor, innovator.*

Your scannable resume must, however, be more than a list of nouns naming job titles you have held *(technical writer),* software you know *(CAD),* or your qualities *(skilled manager).* If the scanning software selects

Box 26.4

ASCII Scannable Resume

Compare this resume with the traditional version in Box 24.5

MARIA STROPPOLO

1536 Ginger Street
Newton, PA 17865
(413) 765-9087
stroppolo@aol.com

KEYWORD SUMMARY
Manager whose innovations led to increased profits. Experienced in employee training, purchasing, bookkeeping. Volunteer work as professional writer. Know DOS/Windows and Mac word-processing software.

EXPERIENCE
Assistant manager for Clarktown, Pennsylvania, Mobile gas station (1996–Present)

—Did paperwork for gasoline and store product sales
—Constructed time-saving process for the daily checkout
—Trained new employees
—Arranged work shifts for new employees

Manager of Bolton's Fish Market, Clarktown, PA (1992–96)

—Supervised 8 employees
—Ordered all products
—Did the bookkeeping
—Opened a lunch bar on the premises, which became very profitable

Volunteer for the Clarktown SENIOR TIMES magazine (1990–present)

—Write responses to inquiries and complaints from subscribers
—Research and write articles at the request of the editor

EDUCATION
B.A. Management, Pumpkinville College, 3.2 QPA
24 credits, Clarkville Junior College, 3.4 QPA

it, a real person will read your scanned ASCII resume. Your resume must appeal to the human mind as well as the computer program. It should make sense, and it should be attractive and easy to read.

If you are printing your scannable resume and mailing it to the employer, avoid these characteristics, which interfere with the scanning process:

- Nonwhite paper
- Dot matrix print
- Italics, underlining, and other font manipulations
- Crowding of text (use white space liberally)
- Exotic fonts (Helvetica is best)
- Small type (use 12 to 14 point).

Box 26.4 provides an example of an ASCII resume design for scanning.

Problems for Classwork and Homework

P26.1 Library Indexes

Use the electronic indexes in your library to find resources related to job search:

a. Find one book and one article; report to the class on what they cover.
b. Create a bibliography of ten entries that includes both books and articles; type it up and submit it to your instructor.

P26.2 Search Engines

Conduct a WWW search for job resources relevant to your major. Use three different search engines (see section 26.3). Report to your class or your instructor on which engine worked best and why.

P26.3 On-Line Databases

Conduct a WWW search for job resources relevant to your major. Use two different databases listed in section 26.3. Report to your class or to your instructor on which database provided the most interesting information and why.

P26.4 Find Job Ads

Using the job-list sites in Box 26.1, find and print out three advertisements for jobs in your specialty.

P26.5 Scannable ASCII resume

Create a scannable ASCII resume targeted at a job advertisement found on the WWW. Attach a copy of the advertisement to your resume when you turn it in.

REFERENCES

Anderson, P. V. (1985). Survey methodology. In L. Odell & D. Goswami (Eds.), *Writing in nonacademic settings* (pp. 453–501). New York: Guildford.

Britton, J., Burgess, T., Martin, N., McLeod, A., & Rosen, H. (1975). *The development of writing abilities (11–18).* Urbana, Il: National Council of Teachers of English.

Cannon, L. (1997, July 21). Prosperity, with a Latin beat. *The Washington Post National Weekly Edition,* p. 33.

Ede, L. (1984). Audience: An introduction to research. *College Composition and Communication, 35,* 140–154.

Ede, L., & Lunsford, A. (1984). Audience addressed / audience invoked: The role of audience in composition theory and pedagogy. *College Composition and Communication, 35,* 155–171.

Faighley, L., & Miller, T.P. (1982). What we learn from writing on the job. *College English, 44,* 557–569.

Fisher, G. (1992). *Mindsets: The role of culture and perception on international relations.* Yarmouth, ME: Intercultural Press, Inc.

Flower, L. (1979). Writer-based prose: A cognitive basis for problems in writing. *College English, 41,* 19–37.

Hall, E. T., & Hall, M. R. (1987). *Hidden differences: Doing business with the Japanese.* NY: Anchor/Doubleday.

Hoey, M. (1983). *On the surface of discourse.* Boston: George Allen & Unwin.

Kirsch, G., & Roen, D. H. (1990). *A sense of audience in written communication.* London: Sage.

Kroll, B.M. (1984). Writing for readers: Three perspectives on audience. *College Composition and Communication, 35,* 172–185.

Lanham, R. (1992). *Revising business prose.* (3rd. ed.). New York: Macmillan.

Leaper, N. (1994, June/July). Ahh . . . the pitfalls of international communication. *Communication World,* 58–60.

Mathes, J. C., & Stevenson, D. W. (1991). *Designing technical reports: Writing for audiences in organizations.* New York: Macmillan.

Webster's Dictionary of English Usage. (1989). Springfield, MA: Merriam-Webster.

Morin, R. (1997, September 1). The worst of the worst. *The Washington Post Weekly Edition,* p. 35.

Murray, D. (1985). *A writer teaches writing* (2nd ed.). Boston: Houghton Mifflin.

Singer, M. R. (1987). *Intercultural communication: A perceptual approach.* Englewood Cliffs, NJ: Prentice-Hall.

Sommers, N. (1980). Revision strategies of student writers and experienced adult writers. *College Composition and Communication, 31,* 378–388.

Zuber, S., & Reed, A. M. (1993). The politics of grammar handbooks: Generic *he* and singular *they. College English, 55,* 515–531.

INDEX